Praise for *Flow*

"In *Flow*, the authors raise some innovative, provocative, and in many instances counter-intuitive ideas on how companies can enhance their supply chain efficiency. This is a very valuable contribution to finding long-term supply chain solutions."

Kevin Brown, Chief Supply Chain Officer, Dell Technologies

"Once again, Linton and Handfield provide great insight for today's C-suite, enabling them to build out actionable pathways for improved supply chain decision-making. The authors' expertise and wisdom is shared throughout the book and is powerful for accelerating the flow and optimizing financial results."

Chris Collier, retired Chief Financial Officer, Flex

"Linton and Handfield continue to challenge conventional supply chain heuristics. Even this deep into the twenty-first century, supply chains are too frequently understood – and managed – as a sequence of transactions. And they are too frequently managed retroactively, in response to events, rather than proactively, anticipating events. Applying principles from the physics of flow systems, the authors argue that our supply networks cannot remain rigid and static, but must evolve over time. This new conceptual approach importantly includes not just anticipating supply disruptions (i.e., supply *risk*) but also understanding changing *demand* signals, an often overlooked element of managing supply networks. Finally, this new way of thinking shifts attention from last century's static financial metric – i.e., *cost*. In this new way of understanding supply systems, the authors focus on *free cash flow*. An emphasis on cost ignores the many other ways in which companies inadvertently destroyed value, by increasing inventories, or ignoring obsolescence, or failing to understand how freight delays extended the cash conversion cycle. In contrast, free cash flow incorporates all these elements of working capital, allowing companies to understand better how their supply ecosystems create value holistically."

Tom Derry, Chief Executive Officer, Institute of Supply Management

"This is the second collaboration between Tom Linton, who has led one of the largest and most complex supply chains in the world, and Rob Handfield, a thoughtful and creative academic. They use the lens of physics to develop powerful insights on important issues in supply chains, like the need for speed, visibility, and localization. This book is an excellent read for anyone who wants to see the supply chain of the future, now."

Marshall L. Fisher, Professor of Operations, Information and Decisions, The Wharton School, University of Pennsylvania

"This is a great read for operations strategists and practitioners alike, who are looking to understand how to think through and navigate complexities of supply chain design. Leaning on creative parallels to fundamental laws that govern science, the book provides great insights into how one should think of optimization and evolution of supply chains in today's world."

Joydeep Ganguly, Chief Operating Officer, Gilead Science

"This is an excellent book all supply chain practitioners should read to survive and thrive in this complex and interconnected world we now live in. There are many great real-life examples which are excellent and relevant."

Daniel Koh, VP Global Strategic Sourcing, HPE

"Supply chain impacts grab the headlines and elevate logistics visibility as a business imperative. In this impressive illumination of the modern supply chain, Tom Linton and Rob Handfield explain the importance of thinking through this global movement of things by addressing the underlying rules that make it work."

Jett McCandless, Founder & CEO, project44

"By recognizing our supply chain's composition, learning its behaviors, and optimizing it responsibly, we can be more resilient to unforeseen challenges and get ahead of discoverable, predictable changes."

Bob Murphy, VP Supply Chain & Chief Procurement Officer, IBM

"Rob Handfield and Tom Linton shed a bright light on the most overlooked reality in the supply chain world: movement is money. This supply chain duo makes a compelling case that we will face big challenges in our increasingly VUCA world, where the physical realities – and physics – of supply chains will be pushed to the limit. A big takeaway is clear: the stakes are high, but the rewards will be great for those who can build and maintain resilient supply chains."

Jason Schenker, Author of *Futureproof Supply Chain* and Chairman of The Futurist Institute

Flow

How the Best
Supply Chains Thrive

Rob Handfield, PhD and Tom Linton

University of Toronto Press
Toronto Buffalo London

Rotman-UTP Publishing
An imprint of University of Toronto Press
Toronto Buffalo London
utorontopress.com

© University of Toronto Press 2022

ISBN 978-1-4875-0832-6 (cloth)
ISBN 978-1-4875-3801-9 (EPUB)
ISBN 978-1-4875-3800-2 (PDF)

Library and Archives Canada Cataloguing in Publication

Title: Flow : how the best supply chains thrive / Rob Handfield, PhD and Tom Linton.
Names: Handfield, Robert B., author. | Linton, Tom (Thomas K.), author.
Description: Includes bibliographical references and index.
Identifiers: Canadiana (print) 20220203199 | Canadiana (ebook) 20220203210 | ISBN 9781487508326 (cloth) | ISBN 9781487538019 (EPUB) | ISBN 9781487538002 (PDF)
Subjects: LCSH: Business logistics. | LCSH: Physical laws.
Classification: LCC HD38.5 .H36 2022 | DDC 658.7 – dc23

We wish to acknowledge the land on which the University of Toronto Press operates. This land is the traditional territory of the Wendat, the Anishnaabeg, the Haudenosaunee, the Métis, and the Mississaugas of the Credit First Nation.

University of Toronto Press acknowledges the financial support of the Government of Canada and the Ontario Arts Council, an agency of the Government of Ontario, for its publishing activities.

Funded by the   Financé par le
Government   gouvernement
of Canada   du Canada

Canada

ONTARIO ARTS COUNCIL
CONSEIL DES ARTS DE L'ONTARIO
an Ontario government agency
un organisme du gouvernement de l'Ontario

For my wife, Sandi Shields
– Rob Handfield

For my wife and lifetime friend, Dr. Cheryl Linton
– Tom Linton

Contents

Preface

Supply chains can be defined as material in motion. Material in motion is cash in motion. Move it fast, and you improve cash flow. Slow it down, and it consumes cash or becomes inventory. Speed it up, and you make customers happier, drive revenue, and improve margins.

What if we thought differently about this movement? What if there were underlying laws that govern good movement versus bad? Can the physics of supply chains be defined and supported by universal truths?

These were some of the questions Rob Handfield and I wrestled with after publishing our first book, *The LIVING Supply Chain*, in 2016. In that book, we took a distinctly biological point of view. We drew parallels to nature as a way of discussing what a good supply chain looks like. We thought, "Is there also a basis in physics?"

The lake I live on in Georgia is more like a pond in size. Yet this small body of water is a waterfowl magnet when the seasons change and birds of all shapes and sizes work their way south or north.

This movement is electric at certain times of the day. It has a rhythm to its flow. Canadian geese and ducks take off and land in a V formation, often telegraphing their coming and going with wonks and quacks in a symphony of sound. Although high in number at times, they never to seem to collide or have any confusion about where they are going or whom to follow. They seem to signal and move in ways that allow them to land and take off safely.

There are exceptions. Every so often, either a predatory eagle or freakish weather limits their movement. They fly point-to-point, searching constantly for food and driven by instincts, environment, or inherited genes, all of which science does not yet fully understand. They have purpose. Their movement is orchestrated and never wasted.

We can learn from birds many things about how things should move. After all, the internet of things has enabled the new movement of things through the access of information from any source, anywhere, at any time. Objects can now signal their presence and other objects can sense it. This data can move globally via the cloud and back to other devices aimed at using it.

That is why we are focusing this book on flow. It is through efficient movement or flow that supply chains thrive. To obtain optimum efficiency, supply chains need to be released from control and allowed to move as freely as possible.

In both the animate and inanimate worlds, we are surrounded by examples of what great supply chains should look like. They are not complex, highly controlled systems but fast, agile, fluid systems that sense, respond, and navigate their way autonomously.

The lesson for business is enormous. Today, weaponized with a set of digital tools, it is possible to achieve new levels of efficiency if we are not supply "chained" and held hostage by processes designed for an analog world. We are living in a world operating in real time, with devices at the edge of the network getting smarter each year. With the emergence of 5G, the internet of things will drive the movement of things to be orchestrated like a flock of geese, a school of fish, or the tributaries that feed a river.

If we look at our existing supply chain world with these optics, we can compress the time it takes to move things. Moreover, we can reduce the cost of doing things and improve financial outcomes throughout the supply chains that move things.

We believe it will be common to see a 2× improvement in supply chain performance when principles of flow are applied with digital tools. When material is moving, cash is moving. Speed it up, and free cash flow, revenue, and customer satisfaction increase, and the cost embedded in friction and resistance is removed.

Flow is how the movement of things will unleash the next evolution in supply chain management.

Tom Linton, January 2022

This book was written during a period of upheaval. We began work almost immediately after publishing our first book, *The LIVING Supply Chain*, when we were inspired to think about the physical flows in nature and how this applies to supply chains. When our first book was released, we were in the early stages of the massive trade war between the United States and China. Something was going on that was not business as usual, and that appeared to be some other shift in the current. Tom Linton spoke at North Carolina State (NC State) University's Supply Chain Resource Cooperative meeting in December 2019, where we further explored the decline of globalization and the possible move toward a localized supply chain world.

Of course, in January 2020, the world economy began to implode rapidly. The coronavirus strains in Wuhan spread quickly and then moved into Italy, Spain, the United States, Mexico, and the rest of the world. In less than four weeks, the economy shifted from a high point in February 2020 to a global economic shutdown that dragged on for many months. As we write this preface in February 2022, the Omicron virus is raging in North America, India, Latin America, and Europe, shutting down flights and businesses. New variants are no doubt imminent. It seems like COVID will be with us for another few years at least, making the world a very different place.

In writing this book, we took inspiration from a famous physicist, Dr. Adrian Bejan, who offered some unique insights that we integrated into a set of ideas related to supply chain flows. This proved to be a very timely topic, as flows of materials have come to a halt in 2021 and 2022, resulting in material shortages and increased price inflation around the world. In the spirit of the constructal law of physics, we discovered that the natural flow of time and events is not all that difficult to predict. This led us to the idea of exploring the nature of supply chain flows – and ultimately, to the underlying vision of creating supply chains that are not so much resilient but immune to shifts in their ecosystem. It has never been more important to begin thinking about how supply chains flow than the current state we find ourselves in today.

In *The LIVING Supply Chain*, we addressed the biological attributes of supply chains and how the essential elements of ecosystems could be used to understand how supply chains operate. In this book, we consider the attributes of supply chains using the physical principals of flow. This theme runs throughout the book, suggesting that there is indeed a natural flow to events in the global supply chain. We employ multiple examples of what we believe are the "best" companies we have worked with and how we can learn from them.

Is this book for you?

Like our previous book, this book relies on multiple case examples, academic theories, and various references related to physical flows, movement, speed, and other relationships that apply. We tried to keep the discussion very practical and focused on the physical properties of supply chains.

The book is targeted at anyone who is curious about how supply chains function and why it is so important that they flow. If supply chains do not flow – and they did not in 2020–22 – huge problems emerge, including product shortages, medical emergencies, and economic shutdowns. We also explore the future of how supply chains are evolving in a post-COVID world. As we noted earlier, we hope our discussion will help people to think differently about how to manage global supply chains in the new era.

There is a lot of press proclaiming the "new digital age" of blockchain, internet of things, artificial intelligence, and an "Industry 4.0" world. But the reality is that many supply chains struggle to flow well and instead are often constrained by many factors. This book is for the rest of us, who live in the real world of daily supply chain management work. As we note in one of our chapters, the best supply chain managers are the ones who tinker with our supply chain propositions and recognize them as truths but then interpret them and innovate to drive something new.

Some of us get lucky and land in a company such as Amazon or Apple. Amazon has a business model that functions with pretty much anything going through it. Apple is blessed with incredible products and a place where spending on new ideas is a part of daily life. But most of us do not work in these places. People also dream of launching a start-up and having an IPO that makes them multi-millionaires, forgetting that more than

50% of start-ups fail in the first five years, and even fewer make it to the IPO level.[1] But this book is about supply chains for the rest of us, who are not blessed with unbelievable amounts of capital, and who put on their boots every day and trudge off to the mine. They are the ones who can take the observations we offer here and start to tinker with them to develop truly innovative supply chains.

As a matter of course, physics provides a number of simple and important laws that are undeniable, irrefutable, and that determine the performance of matter based on stringent formulas and equations. We have couched these physical flows in terms of measures such as speed, distance, electricity, and other phenomena. We have pulled from our own experiences working with companies such as Flex, Honda, Apple, Gilead Science, Biogen, Siemens, Caterpillar, IBM, and others. Each chapter begins with a brief discussion of a physical flow and then interprets each physical flow in terms of a supply chain flow, which helps explain the design and management of supply chains. We believe that a parallel exists between physical flows and supply chain flows that can be used to determine their performance. Each flow is interpreted in terms of a number of supply chain design principles that can be applied to improve simplicity, efficiency, and cost effectiveness.

We have also explored the idea of what it means to create *supply chain immunity*. The idea of immunity is an appealing one – certainly in the COVID age. Immunity implies that the human body has natural antibodies that can fight off invaders and develop independence and self-defense mechanisms that make it not so much resilient but rather safe under fire. An immune response may still be painful; you may still feel sick or unwell, but ultimately your body will recover as all of its resources are put to work to fight off the invading force. We believe this metaphor is useful in designing the supply chains of the future. Sensing mechanisms will be able to detect a threat. Moreover, they will be able to collaborate with self-developing mechanisms that lie within our internal organization and those of our strategic suppliers and customers to fend off the threat and return our enterprises to a normal state. This was certainly not the situation in the US response to COVID and its inability to keep up with the requirements to fend off the invader.[2]

Technologies such as artificial intelligence, blockchain, cognitive computing, machine-based learning, and networked computing are all being highly proclaimed as enablers for the digital transformation that is underway. Although many tout the impact of these technologies that will change supply chains, we disagree. Ultimately, it is the application of these technologies in the context of the physical rules that determine supply chain performance which matters. That is because these emerging technologies often overlook the flow of supply chains, including the fundamental dimensions of time, space, compression, power, waves, and distance. These physical flows can be translated into terms that are essential to running a business in the modern global economy. This book develops a framework and reminds executives that agility in the face of emerging technologies requires that one remain cognizant of the core principles embodied in this metaphor for the current state of supply chains.

This book provides a set of important guidelines that bring the discussion on digital innovation back to earth and remind individuals that there are some foundational principles that can be considered in designing innovative supply chains. Technology will not cure all ills, and a logical, practical perspective grounded in the concept of flow in supply chains provides a more practical perspective for moving forward. Each chapter concludes with some words of wisdom that we believe can help aspiring managers consider how to adopt their supply chain design to the post-COVID global economy.

One of the key ideas we propose is that the steady pursuit of labor cost arbitrage has created global supply chains that must be re-thought. These supply chains are slower, more complex, and harder to manage, and business has now hit the pause button on this rush to globalize offshore. Escalation of the tariff and trade wars between the United States and China is, in our opinion, a singular case that is part of a move toward increasing localization of supply bases and last-mile logistics. These rules can help guide sound insights for practitioners to consider when developing supply chain strategy.

We seek to target not just supply chain executives for this book but also finance executives, who have become more aware of the importance of free cash flow as a key harbinger of business performance and shareholder value. Many early proponents of low-cost country sourcing focused on operational costs at the expense of working capital, and this book emphasizes how the principles of supply chain physics impact financial performance and in particular working capital. To this end, the book will have broader appeal not only to supply management executives but to strategic business leaders as well as human resources, information technology, and innovation managers.

Rob Handfield, February 18, 2022

CHAPTER ONE

Supply Chain Flows and Immunity

I have never been a fan of resiliency as it is often used in supply chain management. Resiliency that slows down supply chains or controls supply chains is the enemy of speed, flow, and positive financial improvement. Today, we have tools that can penetrate deep into supply chains and map their movement. By seeing deeply into supply chains, we don't need to harden them for unknown impacts; we can navigate around problems that otherwise would hurt us. Supply chains must move to be successful, so making them flow is the overall rule we must follow.

Tom Linton, former Chief Supply Chain Officer, Flex

Nature has to flow freely, just like the pandemic has to spread and flow. I recognize that this thinking will not save lives, but it is going to happen because of the evolutionary flow of nature.

Adrian Bejan, Physicist, Duke University

This book will not meet your needs if you are expecting lots of formulas and edicts about lean manufacturing, theory of constraints, minimum order quantities, just-in-time inventory, or other popular topics. You can find a good discussion of these topics in an undergraduate textbook, which one of us has written. Instead, this book adopts a much more conceptual approach to understanding whether underlying sets of patterns, flows, and rhythms exist behind the apparent chaos of supply chains as we know them today, especially in the era of COVID. These flows are not apparent to most of us, who simply expect products to show up magically on shelves, or who explain away the chaos and uncertainty as something we must learn to live with.

We offer an alternative explanation: if, in fact, underlying flows can explain how events occur in global supply chains, then managers can analyze such flows to better predict and plan their supply chains. Think of supply chain problems as a kind of virus and of how medical researchers investigate how viruses spread based on biology, public health measures, and the mathematics of exponential growth. If we can predict, map out, and understand the laws governing supply chains, then we can begin to develop a "vaccine" to combat supply chain problems. Armed with this vaccine, we can develop supply chains that can become more immune to disturbances that result in economic disruption. In effect, we can develop "antibodies" to combat "infections" in global economies. Intriguing!

The events of 2019–22 helped us understand supply chain issues not as random events but as an evolutionary flow of events. Viewed in hindsight, supply chain disruptions may even be predictably based on the laws of probability. We do not mean to imply that we have discovered a cure-all for the myriad problems facing enterprises today in the face of pandemics and trade wars; however, we believe that by scrutinizing such events through the lens of physical flows, we can make more sense of them. This new knowledge can lead us to better ways of thinking about our supply chains and being more prepared in the future. This can help to avoid many of the chronic shortages supply chains faced in 2021 and 2022. These solutions won't be easy and will require investments – however, they can create more immune supply chains to fight back the many uncertainties that lie ahead.

When we first proposed a book on the physical flows of supply chains, we got odd looks from some experts in the field. The laws of physics are relatively immutable, explored and codified over centuries of scientific experimentation and discovery. They have been dutifully memorized by high school and undergraduate physics students.

In contrast, supply chains are huge, complex networks composed of enterprises, information systems, material handling, and contractual relationships. They shift continuously, seemingly at the mercy of unpredictable global events. Multiple tomes and articles have been written about how to manage them. They are generated by human beings, after all. However, just as physics has principles, so do supply chains. The principles underlying physical flows that describe natural events can be extended to understand how flows evolve in supply chains and how supply chain principles can be used to render these systems more immune to unexpected events.

In exploring the parallels between physical and supply chain flows, we consulted physicist Adrian Bejan, a professor of mechanical engineering and materials science at Duke University. Dr. Bejan provides insight into the complexity of nature in general and describes how physical flows can be viewed as an organic system that can be predicted. Bejan's work in the law of evolutionary design, known as the *constructal law*, and other physical laws lead to insights into how complex supply chains evolve. Just as water surges onto a flood plain, then levels off, eventually settling onto lower ground, apparent chaos in global supply chains also follows patterns of surge and recession. In a way similar to how water flows in a natural path, managers in 2020 became "woke" to the concept that supply chain flows are central to surviving in a global economy. If people do not design their supply chains to flow properly, along the lines of the laws of physics, their organizations will not survive. Organizational survival is a function of awareness of how flows of material and information occur in global supply chains.

Our last book, *The LIVING Supply Chain*, advanced the notion that supply chains are biological systems that function much like the ecosystems in the Serengeti region of Tanzania. We introduced the concept of trophic cascades, noting the importance of keeping the system in balance. Every species – from the ant, to the grass, the grass feeders, the carnivores, and even scavengers – plays an important role in keeping the entire system balanced and functioning. When any single member of the food chain is eliminated, the whole system is thrown off kilter. We applied this thinking to the functional ecosystem found in supply chains, noting that material, information, and financial transactions must be kept flowing, forming the lifeblood of these truly living supply chain systems. We also explained how a supply chain can become a body with DNA to track events in its natural ecosystem and can acquire an immune system.

The idea of supply chain immunity is strongly related to the idea of flow. A supply chain immune system works in much the same way that the body's immune system recognizes and eliminates invaders. One's body has an innate immune system[1] that is active from the moment of birth. When the body recognizes an invader, the immune system takes action immediately, sending "warrior" cells called *phagocytes* to surround and kill the invader. Another immune system, called the *acquired immune system*, produces antibodies that protect the body from a specific invader. These antibodies are developed by cells called *B lym-phocytes* after the body has been exposed to the invader. Once exposed to a threat, such as a virus, the immune system recognizes that particular threat and defends the body against it. This is what immunization does: it trains the immune system to make antibodies to protect against harmful diseases.

Then what do we mean by supply chain immunity? Imagine describing supply chains in terms of their flows. Managers can create demand- and risk-sensing capabilities at the right points in these flows, as well as alerts and plans to prepare for events that can disrupt or alter these flows.

The laws of biology and the physical laws of nature and their relationships to supply chains play an important role in framing the concepts of this book. As we began to think about what is happening in today's supply chain systems, it became clear that a few critical variables are at play. Akin to biological laws, these variables mimic the properties of physical phenomena, specifically the ways one's body develops immunity to viruses and infectious diseases. And just like the physical laws of nature, mass, motion, and time are critical components that also define supply chains. All the elements of supply chains – cash, inventory, and information – can be defined in terms of both their motion and the time associated with the beginning and end of that motion.

What is the most important metric governing physical supply chains? Free cash flow. It is key to every job. Supply chains can be characterized as material in motion. Stated another way, supply chains are cash in motion. The fundamental law of supply chain flows is that faster movement of materials is better than slower movement. The faster cash moves in the echelons of a supply chain, the faster free cash flow is generated for a business in a defined period of time.

We advance the notion here that free cash flow can also define unhealthy supply chains. When the blood is not flowing well in a human body, the cells cannot fight invaders as well as they should. When material is sitting in inventory instead of moving, it cannot generate free cash and thus loses value. The laws of motion derived from first principles of physics can help us understand why material is not moving and why it is sitting still.

Another important and related factor involves distance, which determines relative speed and acceleration. By studying how the laws of time, motion, and distance apply to supply chain phenomena such as cash, material, and information, we can begin to derive the key laws that frame ways to design more effective supply chains. We need supply chains that are more autonomous, can better sense demand, and are less dependent on human response.

We will demonstrate how the ongoing evolution in supply chain flows has important implications for how managers can observe and exploit these flows to manage supply chains. We provide evidence for these insights gleaned from many years of working with leading enterprises, observing managers in action, and in some cases tying ideas to the metaphor of natural physical flows. Global supply chains have been around for thousands of years, going back to China's Silk Road. The post-COVID world will likely see supply chains evolve in response to the new ecosystems imposed on them. In this book, we imagine how these evolved supply chains will unfold.

The world we knew in 2019 became forever changed in 2020. Although global supply chains have grown more efficient through improvements in software technologies, cloud computing, and mobilization, many business processes have been forced to rapidly adapt and innovate in a post-COVID world. Disruptions shut down many businesses. Lack of consumer demand left products stranded, rejected, or heavily discounted. Bloated inventories had to be written off as obsolete. Capacity imbalances in different tiers caused shortages, booms, and busts across multiple industries, generating lawsuits and invoking force majeure clauses. Frequent product shortages became the norm, especially in healthcare, food, pharmaceuticals, and electronics. The US national stockpile was woefully unprepared to deal with the onslaught of the pandemic in hospital intensive care units (ICUs).[2]

Compared to the physical world, which has evolved over millions of years, our modern supply chains are at an infantile stage. We can certainly do better, and the opportunity for improvements in supply chain design, structure, and buyer-seller relationships is massive. Using the natural world as a source of inspiration, we can see how even the smallest detail has adapted to changing circumstances over time and continues to adapt. Events like the coronavirus will catalyze a new spurt of adaptations in supply chain design.

Supply chain management is about getting things moving; that applies not only to roads, airports, and ships but to how we think about getting things to people. Companies such as Amazon have constructed massive distribution centers near major hubs, including Los Angeles, Atlanta, New York, St. Louis, Raleigh, and Chicago, with direct access to on-ramps to interstate highways built in the 1950s. We not only need to leverage what is already in place but to ask ourselves how we would design an optimal supply chain from scratch. How do we design supply chains that not only result in the lowest cost but that flex under pressure? How can we ensure that they do the least damage to our environment by reducing fuel consumption and preserving biodiversity?

Just as palmettos flex and lose only a few leaves in hurricane-force winds while pine trees snap, our supply chains must bend to withstand the storms of major pandemics and financial systems implosion. Many experts talk about creating supply chain resilience.[3] Instilling a supply chain's resilience by carrying a lot of inventory and retaining wasteful redundancies is like surrounding a pine tree's roots with concrete and inserting a steel pole into its trunk to make sure it does not break. This solution is inefficient, costly, and ultimately harmful to enterprises. A better way is to apply the laws of physics and biology to create supply chain immunity.

Physical Supply Chain Flows Are Not a New Idea

We are not the first to note the importance of physical flows as a means for assessing supply chain performance. Most supply chain textbooks focus largely on mathematical formulas that define performance and on internal factory operations. While such formulas are an important contribution, we seek a more generalized approach. We explore how to apply physical principles to the global supply chain and note how to consider strategic levers in light of the overall principles of supply chain flow. Our goal is to observe how supply chains – particularly global ones – flow in a way that mirrors physical flows and is not directly tied to mathematical formulas.

This book explains how supply chain flows relate to critical strategic decisions about how to configure and operate business processes for the next decade. In effect, the laws of motion and first principles can be used as guideposts for making decisions about logistics, network design, strategic sourcing, factory location, workforce management and training, and a host of other key functions. We will also explore the impact of supply chain flows on global market policies, such as tariffs, factory location, supply-based geographies, value-added business processes, and outsourcing.

Several unique elements differentiate our book's approach from those of other books on supply chain analytics and physics. First, traditional supply chain books deal with a common set of themes, such as increased disruptions in the supply chain, use of big data, and network optimization and they tend to focus on cost minimization. But this is the first book to explore the application of physical principles regarding flow.

Many recent books targeted to a wide audience talk about using data to drive customer analytics and better market value.[4] Others address risk and disruption through improved resiliency.[5] More technical supply chain books focus on how to design supply chains to reduce risk.[6] We are not the first authors to apply physical laws to supply chains. For instance, *Factory Physics*[7] targets academics and students; it focuses on the factory.

While these books are certainly relevant, they effectively observe that our world is complicated and risky. Organizations build collaborative clusters that provide incremental benefits to all parties involved, and static data can be used to target customers and optimize cost savings. These observations are somewhat interesting to business professionals but, in effect, are not novel.

Finally, many current supply chain books advocate traditional approaches to improving supply chains. These approaches involve becoming leaner, forming more long-term and collaborative approaches with suppliers, using analytics to exploit the internet of things, and driving innovation in product development through partnerships with other firms. Again, these principles are prescribed in many books, but in our experience, they are not well-executed by most organizations.

This book concentrates on physical supply chain flows that span multiple operations and potentially several countries or continents. It broadens the factory physics concept to reflect the shifting nature of roles played by a range of enterprises and entities in the global supply chain network. Rather than presenting physical principles in the form of mathematical formulas, we describe a set of fundamental truths and relationships that we have observed in physical supply chains using evidence drawn from our own experience. We offer specific examples of supply chain flows at work: pragmatic stories, experiences, and observations gleaned from our individual careers.

Another important observation we make is that a gradual but noticeable evolution has already begun in supply chains worldwide. Specifically, our supply chain structures are beginning to become less globalized and more localized. This theme, woven into several chapters, aligns with our belief in the need to speed up supply chain flows by focusing on velocity, a concept discussed in our prior book. The localization theme is consistent with the theme of creating supply chains that are immune to disruptions. As discussed in chapter 4, flows are easier to predict when they are closer and more compressed.

We hope both to challenge practitioners on their fundamental assumptions and to inspire them to apply new ways of thinking about how supply chains can be run. We encourage practitioners to focus on the ways in which geographic proximity improves speed, rather than sticking with globalized supply chains that offer lower supply cost but are slower and require large working capital balances. It will be useful to explore how to apply natural principles in our current atmosphere around tariffs, anti-dumping, and countervailing duties. Numerous examples of how physical flows apply to real-life business situations will come alive to our readers.

We draw on these principles to make recommendations to our readers on how to become better prepared for evolutionary flows occurring in supply chains. In doing so, we have relied on extensive interactions with senior executive leaders; in-depth case studies, detailed workshops, and forums; as well as published research in this area. The physical laws espoused by Dr. Bejan, introduced earlier, are also critical to our findings.

Technology Does Not Drive Supply Chain Innovation

Many organizations focus on employing technology to drive competitive advantage in their supply chains. We adopt a somewhat different focus on technologies that provide advantages attributable to key physical metrics. For example, we can use the key metric of free cash flow to indicate three important factors: the financial health of the company, customer satisfaction, and the likelihood of repeat business. Free cash flow is the new metric for assessing how business speed and financial performance are linked. It is extremely important to multiple business stakeholders, not only those in supply chain roles but in finance, IT, human resources, and innovation management. The physics of supply chains are foundational to the application of artificial intelligence, cognitive computing, augmented reality, blockchain, and other new technologies. This is because in corporations, every decision is rooted in whether it produces a financial advantage. Speed, compression, and the other laws of supply chain physics all have direct relationships to financial performance, specifically to working capital and free cash flow. Executives who ignore the physical laws of supply chains do so at their peril.

Over the last 30 years, executives in multiple industries (starting with GE's Jack Welch, who initiated this shift) began moving all their manufacturing operations offshore to China, India, Eastern Europe, and other countries with low-cost labor. This became a labor arbitrage game, where the goal was to push costs lower and to drive margins and profits higher. In effect, it became a race to the bottom. As a result, supply chains became increasingly extended, with longer lead times, more inventory and delays, less communication, and the loss of intellectual property. Many companies' balance sheets went a bit haywire: their working capital and pipeline inventory became bloated, supply lead times went from weeks to months, and the volume of damaged goods and excess/obsolete inventory escalated. Eventually, as overhead costs rose, customer satisfaction suffered, costs began to rise, and the lower labor cost of outsourced products became less of an advantage.

The drive to reduce costs and satisfy the demand for increased operating income has become less appealing in the post-globalization era. Applying the principles of supply chain physics increasingly reveals that organizations have sacrificed distance, time, and speed, making the business case for globalization less appealing. Political events, such as Brexit, Trump's tariffs on China and declining to join the Trans Pacific Partnership, along with the growth of the Regional Comprehensive Economic Partnership (RCEP), all point to the shift toward localized supply chains. Other forces, including regionalism, nationalism, and the loss of intellectual property, have made the cost differential associated with a globalization strategy less compelling as the costs between different geographies are also shrinking. It is more complicated for a US business to run a factory in Bangladesh, India, or China than it is, say, in Nebraska. The following chapters emphasize how these physical laws (distance, time, and speed) will have a greater impact in the next decade.

How Physical Laws Apply to Supply Chain Principles

Physics is integral to what happens around us every day. Physical flows provide an underlying set of rules that explain why things around us happen the way they do. The universal nature of these physical principles makes them inherently appealing; engineers use them to design products, processes, and systems and rely on them to hold true in various situations. Physics governs the behavior of matter, time, and space, making it critical in mechanics and industrial design as well as in the construction, electrical, chemical, and nuclear power industries.

As such, we derive a set of principles for supply chain flows that can be applied to what we see happening in global supply chains in our post-COVID world. The parallel between physical and supply chain flows is eloquently depicted by Dr. Bejan. He writes in *The Physics of Life*: "The way to see the law of physics of living systems is to see them as flow systems in motion, driven by power, with finite-size constraints and above all, with freedom to change and time direction for the evolution of design changes."[8]

Physics depicts the evolutionary path of every natural entity in terms of freedom and thermodynamics. This principle is especially suited to thinking about the ways in which supply chains morph and develop. We will return to this principle several times throughout this book.

Among the most obvious physical properties that relate to supply chains are distance and time. Shipping a container to the United States can take 30 days on a vessel from Shanghai or one day on a truck from Mexico. In an era of global trade shifts, distance is becoming an ever-more-important variable in supply chain planning. This book delves deeply into the physical attributes of distance and time and how they affect the supply chain.

Weight and volume are also critical. Increases in either one will naturally increase shipping cost: higher volumes, weight, and distance take more time and cost more. This leads to interesting discussions about the cost of shipping quickly versus the cost of holding material for a longer time in transit. For instance, buying products in China may result in a lower price that improves the company's operating margin. However, because of the long transit time, inventory sits on the balance sheet longer and weighs down the company's working capital. This transit time from China through Los Angeles expanded from six weeks to more than twelve weeks in 2021 due to the constraints at the Los Angeles/Long Beach port, and shippers began having to consider alternative routes, in some cases through Panama up to East Coast ports. Considering such trade-offs involves understanding the landed cost of pursuing globalization. Of course, if the product has very high value and low volume, such as an Apple iPhone, it makes sense to put it on a plane for a longer distance and pay a higher freight cost. Apple will do this if it is running late on a product announcement and will suck up a lot of airlift to get its phones to the market on time. But most organizations will put heavy, bulky, or low-value products on a ship. Even then, there are exceptions, such as when the US government shipped N95 masks by air freight in 2020 through "Operation Air Lift." During COVID, the cost of booking a single plane out of China to the US grew to more than $1M for a single flight.

The physical properties of material are critical in supply chains, and although the physical rules come into play somewhat, we are not particularly concerned with them in this book. Instead of focusing on how physical rules impact our surroundings, we focus on the *application* of physical rules.

For example, supply chains and logistics have had a big impact on military history. Military strategy evolved from the formal era of Napoleon to the more free-form structure of the Civil War, in which attacks occurred from wooded areas. It changed again from trench warfare in World War I, to tank warfare in World War II, to guerilla tactics in Afghanistan. Over time, military powers learned to become more agile and to operate in different ways. Many significant battles were lost because foolish generals ignored critical intelligence and relied on their instincts. That is what happened to Napoleon in the battle of Waterloo (1815) and to Lord Cardigan of Great Britain in the Charge of the Light Brigade (1854).[9] Military powers now seek to create an agile force that makes small, quick, targeted attacks. These forces respond constantly to up-to-date field intelligence that will give them a momentary advantage in combat.

Military logistics also played a role in how transportation evolved. Trains were originally designed to move military troops, and the United States built its interstate highway system to move troops and weapons more efficiently to repel a potential foreign invasion. The ability to physically move soldiers and material has been the differentiator in most military campaigns, and it is often critical to a battle's success or failure.

This is not to say that physical laws are all that matters. Clearly culture – encompassing social communities, work ethic, educational institutions, infrastructure, and governments – also enables every supply chain to adapt to the global ecosystem. In short, culture enables a country's supply chain to flow. Cultures also must embrace change to survive. Singapore's leaders, for example, recognized that their country's geographic location could play a role in the global logistics system. They set up their country as a logistics center, building ports and infrastructure and pivoting the country's economy to improve its supply chain efficiency for transportation and business. Similarly, when FedEx chose to build its headquarters in Memphis, the city's entire culture shifted to embrace this industry, leading to the growth of distribution centers, factories, and warehouses in the area. These two examples are not anomalies. Throughout history, major logistics hubs (cities located along major trading routes) have embraced change to enable supply chain and economic success. In a sense, an enabling culture is the key lubricant that creates the flow, versus the friction, that enables physical laws to act. An adaptable culture enables flow, whereas a resistant culture, such as a community lobbying against Amazon's plans to build a headquarters in New York City, can stop physical progress in its tracks.

In a recent meeting with the son of the Crown Prince in Dubai, Tom Linton was asked, "What is the singular most important thing that Dubai could do to improve its economy?" "The one thing you could do ... is to build a railway across Africa, starting in Dubai and ending at the coast of Mali," Linton replied.

Such a railway would enable the efficient movement of material across the continent, with a 48-hour transportation window as opposed to five days by ship around the continent. There is just one problem with the railway idea: Sudan, which does not have a stable government and would likely not function well as a conduit for goods. But if one could enable the flow of material across Africa, Dubai's economy could skyrocket. That is how the culture of flow works. In referring to culture's relationship with physical supply chains, we refer to society, economies, work ethic, education, and all other components that allow flow to occur.

To overcome the complexity of today's operating environment, it is essential to understand and embrace the natural flows of global supply chain commerce. This means overcoming resistance to change with force and influence, and if that resistance is too heavy to move, applying leverage to lift it. This book emphasizes the importance of solution design, which requires rethinking assumptions about data, flow, and how people learn. There are no simple formulas for how to embrace flow. Every company will need to learn how to observe and understand what natural evolutionary flows mean in terms of their particular goals, corporate culture and philosophy, and executive team's flexibility. This will require challenging assumptions and taking risks with innovative ways to align decision-making in an evolving supply chain.

An Overview of the Book

This chapter introduced the basic idea that when the supply chain does not flow, there is a problem. We seek to explore how to improve the flows that exist in global supply chains and to illuminate how problems can occur, using examples and observations. We will also examine supply chain flows using parallels from the world of physics, including time and velocity, force, pressure, throughput, capacity, electrical flows, and the stability of physical systems.

Chapter 2 explores the fundamental property that comes up in physics again and again: time. Velocity, a calculation of the distance an object travels in a given amount of time, is especially relevant to supply chain mechanics. Other important time-linked ratios include force and time, work and time, and changes that occur over time.

How do these physical laws relate to the supply chain? In the electronics sector, for example, the takedown curve of cost means that components drop in value at a rate of around eight percent per year because the technology becomes obsolete quickly. For this reason, speed is critical to managing supply chains: acting quickly and avoiding holding material in inventory is paramount. If one buys dynamic random access memory (DRAM) chips in the summer, their value will have reduced by 10 percent by Christmas. If the chips are not packaged and shipped, the inventory will have a lower value at the end of the year. However, with the semiconductor shortage this year, the takedown in cost has reversed direction, and chips have become a precious commodity prized for their rarity, particularly in automotive-related industries.

Chapter 3 examines the evolution of supply chains, mirroring the physical principles of thermodynamics. Thermodynamics, a major component of physics, is expressed in the form of constructal law, which sets out the natural design laws governing evolution. In essence, we propose that supply chain flows follow the principles of evolutionary design. We can extend this thinking to better understand how to model flows in a supply chain to predict outcomes. If one agrees that free flow is better than restricted flow, then attention to the way data flows through an organization is integral to its digital dexterity. Dr. Bejan's research focuses on flows in nature, noting that everything flows toward freedom. Rivers flow to the ocean, and all matter flows toward an end state, whether governed by the lowest gravitational pull or the natural pull of wind and geography. A company must understand the flow of its ecosystem to predict evolutionary outcomes and enable executives to develop strategies that consider how its markets and partners will evolve.

Chapter 4 continues to explore constructal law but focuses on the laws of compression and the increasing tendency to evolve toward supply chain localization, drawing on the lessons of trade wars and the fallout from COVID. We offer case studies showing how distance prevents quick response and showing the need for cultural localization and relationship management. The latter is key to effectively integrating supply chains and to continuous improvement. These case studies emphasize the need for improved buyer-seller integration, a topic covered in a full-day meeting of the Supply Chain Resource Cooperative in December 2019. We will integrate insights from multiple executives who emphasize that as we diminish face-to-face interactions due to social distancing, we need to devise new approaches for development and sustenance of supply chain relationships. These approaches are key to driving continuous improvement, cost savings, and innovation in the supply chain.

Chapter 5 explores the concept of stability in physical systems and how supply chain immunity in the face of diverse shocks to the system can be achieved. We explore how information systems can reduce decision-making time, allowing a much quicker response to small changes in the supply chain ecosystem. This chapter also addresses the role of human beings in the decision-making loop, particularly in regard to situational analysis.

Chapter 6 draws on the laws of electrical current and explains how physical principles describe how electricity flows through networked systems. We employ the metaphor that visibility is critical for ensuring that information flows between supply chain partners like electricity in a series circuit. However, visibility must be accompanied by a set of guidelines and philosophies that allows organizations in the supply chain to interact and to resolve conflicts. These guidelines must also allow for new information that the system is not trained to deal with.

Chapter 7 concludes with insights for the future, using the lessons learned from constructal and physical laws on evolutionary flows. We reflect on how supply chain evolutionary flows can be used to predict the shape of future supply chains in a post-COVID world, leading to greater immunity to future shocks. We offer recommendations for managers on how to consider the pattern of flows in creating greater organizational immunity to disruptions. These predictions are meant to spur thinking and debate and provide a basis for considering new possibilities in the new normal.

CHAPTER TWO

Time, Velocity, and Immunity

From knowledge comes foresight, from foresight comes action.[1]

Auguste Comte

Physics dictates that time flows in one direction and points in the direction of the changes that will occur. Likewise in supply chains, the arrow of time indicates the evolution of flow in an organization over time. Managers who become aware of time flows will be better at predicting and managing the evolution of events in their supply chains, allowing them to take action based on this information. Knowledge of the time vector is key to driving competitive advantage, according to Comte, a nineteenth-century French philosopher known as the founder of positivism.

Previous supply chain thinking has emphasized the flow of time as a core component of supply chain performance. Organizations such as Amazon created an entire industry, using time as their competitive weapon, by promising same- or next- day deliveries.

Velocity was also a key objective of the Flex Corporation when Tom Linton was its chief supply chain officer. Flex created the Pulse, a company-wide mobility system that created visual representations of all material flows in Flex's 180-factory network.[2] The resulting change in culture and behavior in the organization was revolutionary. The Pulse created immediate transparency into the flows of all parts of the business and became the "North Star" that guided all ensuing action. This transparency made all business flows visible. It meant that all executives were immediately accountable; they could no longer hide or make excuses for delays in material flow.

Transparent business flows introduced a new way of operating at Flex. The new transparency even sparked debates between the finance and legal teams about whether confidentiality was being breached. Once inaccuracies and blame for flow blockages were eliminated, the gravitational pull of time vectors became evident to everyone. This change enabled materials to flow more freely and to the right places. With flow friction reduced, materials also moved more quickly.

A high level of transparency ensured that leaders were immediately aware of the time vector for material flows across their customer supply chains. As a result, they could become immediately aware of time delays (barriers to flow) and act more quickly to solve them. Imagine Flex as a riverboat and its executives as the crew. If the crew can spot a logjam ahead and send someone out to break up the jam, the water will move unimpeded, carrying the riverboat downriver faster. Armed with the knowledge that logs tend to jam at a particular spot in the river, the crew might redesign its route to avoid that spot or work with loggers to ensure that logs do not jam at that spot in the future. Riverboat re-routing could be likened to revising a company's system design. Executives/crew gain a greater understanding of the physical limitations of the infrastructure/river being used to support the flow. This new knowledge drives investment in other equipment or capital that can further enhance flow and velocity.

Velocity, a function of time and distance, is one of many time vectors that is of interest to physicists. In physics, the ability to increase velocity will affect any number of desired outcomes. The same is true for supply chain outcomes. The fact is, doing anything faster is generally better because there are relatively few downsides to increasing the speed of movement of materials or completion of services in supply chains. This universal concept has become central to many executive boardroom discussions that focus on financial outcomes, many of which are related to improved velocity. Think of the following financial flows that are velocity-related:

- Many global supply chains focus on working capital (as opposed to profit margin) as a key measure of performance. Working capital is the most obvious outcome of increased velocity of a company's financial flow as cash flow speeds up over time.
- Improving asset velocity, and specifically ensuring that inventory is constantly moving, is critical to a healthy supply chain.
- Velocity of planning and execution can produce improved outcomes, including better customer service, increased inventory turns, greater agility in response to change, and quicker reaction time to supply chain disruptions.
- Velocity of decision-making in the face of major supply chain disruptions can significantly reduce the impact of a major disaster, as acting quickly based on real-time information can mitigate potential disasters.

A company's ability to act quickly based on early notification of events is critical to creating an important organizational resource for the future: supply chain immunity. As described in chapter 1, we define *supply chain immunity* as the capability of an organization to detect changes in its ecosystem, recognize the shift in conditions, and respond in an agile manner to accommodate these shifts. Given how the flows of nature occur, a company's ability to detect signals and act quickly before a disaster strikes, its network shuts down, or a disruptive event takes place is more critical than ever. In a post-COVID world, how do we develop the capabilities to optimize and design supply chains based not just on lowest cost, as we have done previously, but on the abilities to flex under pressure and operate under duress?

Supply chain immunity is an organization's ability to survive in the face of massive disruptions of products and services in its supply chain. However, many of us working in supply chains have noticed that it is not enough to know where the disruption is occurring; it is essential to know what to do in an emergency. What this means is having a playbook that presents a plan for how to respond, that provides guidelines for people to follow when something unexpected happens. It should be general enough to cover any potential threat. We also need to know how to minimize the potential effects of supply chain failures from shutting us down should a major global event like a pandemic affect us. What we need is a plan for ongoing and persistent immunity.

Two of the primary requirements for supply chain immunity are the very elements we discussed earlier: visibility and velocity. Let's explore this further.

Because of the rapid succession of events during the COVID crisis, the need for real-time supply chain information has never been clearer. People working at home need to see what is happening in their supply chains right now and need to review this data with others to reach immediate consensus on how to deal with unexpected disruptions. Real-time data leads to action plans on how to deal with new crises and disruptions. Although many digital supply chain tools have been adopted in recent years, they are only as good as the timeliness of the data that are presented in them. A look backwards is unlikely to be helpful. Think of looking at a speedometer on your car as you drive down the road. You need to know how fast you are going right now, not five minutes ago.

But organizations also need to train managers on how to make decisions using real-time data. This means creating a culture where managers are not afraid of making a decision based on this data, or what is often called the *hinge factor*. A hinge factor is a defining moment, decision, or event that turns the tables and ultimately affects the flow of events in a battle, society, or supply chain.[3] In the case of Flex, the Pulse created hinge factors for all managers, who had to learn how to make decisions using real-time data. Flex's new ability to see what was happening in its supply chain involved a cultural transformation that required managers to rapidly absorb information and adapt to environmental shifts.

A greater number of organizations are investing in systems that produce real-time data on changing situations, allowing managers to respond to this data more quickly. For instance, the Resilinc[4] platform provides rapid updates on events occurring near an organization's major distribution centers and supplier network. It can rapidly notify managers of a disruptive event and the net financial impact of a disruption on other nodes (physical entities or planning points) in the supply chain. This increased intelligence is equivalent to having accurate, up-to-date intelligence in a battlefield. But knowing what to do with that information is critical, and Resilinc cannot tell you that. As Eric Durschmied points out in *The Hinge Factor*, it also requires generals in battle, as well as managers in the field, to understand what to do with the intelligence. Knowledge without action is a choice that is often viewed with regret in hindsight.

Improving Asset Velocity – Material Flows over Time

Moving material quickly through a supply chain and making rapid decisions based on quick responses surely sounds desirable and, as we have noted, can provide increased immunity to shocks in the ecosystem. But what prevents organizations from doing more of this? What is the holdup?

Our analysis of many organizations over the years reveals that the answer often lies in the lack of governance that surrounds supply chain flows across an organization's hierarchies and functions. As it turns out, three company actions are critical to successful inventory velocity. The first is assigning responsibility for generating material from the outset of a product's life cycle. The second is designing products for life cycle management considering how material and components will flow in the process. The third is improving communication between sales and supply chain planning teams, which is also fundamental to asset velocity. Improved communication leads to better planning and coordination between suppliers and end customers.

In effect, inventory that is not in motion creates friction, the opposite of flow. Inventory sitting still becomes a cash consumer instead of a cash producer. Shrinking the distance between factories, suppliers, and customers reduces the time needed to move materials between them and the space between the nodes. Companies become leaner by removing waste from manufacturing and increasing the velocity of movement of materials between parties in the supply chain. In this sense, lean supply chains are interwoven with the laws of physics.

Barriers That Prevent Inventory from Flowing Naturally

When inventory gets bogged down, it stops moving altogether. In some cases, inventory can sit for many years before being discovered and either sold as scrap or thrown away. There is an accounting term for this unfortunate state of affairs: excess inventory and obsolete materials, often called E&O. It is the scourge of many supply chain managers, and it is worthwhile to examine the reasons E&O even exists.

In a recent workshop at NC State University,[5] executives discussed why inventory flows were being shut down, which often resulted in inventory being thrown away or sold at a discount, ultimately creating costs. Managers at this workshop came from many different industries, including pharmaceuticals, electronics, chemicals, automotive, and industrial. No matter what context, all managers identified common reasons for why inventory stopped flowing over time. Slow-moving inventory was often a by-product of misaligned decisions in areas such as product life cycles, design standardization, and promotional sales forecasting incentives. It was common to find that the cost of excess inventory was often not measured effectively and therefore often ignored on balance sheets. A root cause was the lack of communication between sales and operations forecasting, which led to a pileup of inventory that often had to be written off at the end of each business cycle.

To prevent excess inventory write-offs, companies should document the individual components of inventory cost, including labor (warehouse management), damage, carrying cost, liability insurance, contractual obligation costs, and other factors. The goal of doing so is not to drive accountability or blame but to ensure that everyone – including sales, manufacturing, and purchasing/suppliers – is aware of the cost of poor inventory decisions.

Inventory also piles up when a product is phased out or when a capital project concludes. Contractual commitments for holding inventory are often not well-defined, and the cost of customer commitments is often not factored into the sales account management cycle.

When functional groups do not effectively work together to plan business cycles, inventory problems are sure to follow. Even within sales and operations, different locations may be buying the same materials but not sharing information. One division may have $10 million worth of inventory, while another is chasing down material to produce the same part.

Every industry seems to have an inventory problem, which is often misunderstood and understated. For example, a $4 billion company believed its total excess inventory was valued at $4 million. However, a study of the company discovered more than $44 million of excess inventory in its warehouses. Most of the company's material was obsolete, with stacks of 10-year-old materials that company executives did not even know was there.

Another problem, of course, is the misalignment that occurs during product planning cycles when forecasts are developed. Most companies do not want to lose a sale, so inventory left over at the end of a quarter is often viewed as a mistake. When excess inventory occurs, it is frequently not acknowledged, and the decision on what to do with it is kicked forward into the future. Eventually, the sins of the company fall on the supply chain, and the excess inventory becomes the property of the supply chain team.

Companies should examine and employ the approaches described above to promote increased velocity of their working capital inventory. Doing so may require significant changes in company mindset and culture but can produce important outcomes. First among these changes is eliminating the hoarding mentality of some executives, who feel uncomfortable if they are not sitting on a pile of inventory. Even during the supply chain shortages of 2021, companies had excess inventory; however, they were holding all the wrong types of materials, and not what customers were demanding!

The Constructal Law

The topic of slow-moving material shows up in laws of physics, as expressed by Dr. Bejan in his constructal law:

> For a finite-size flow system to persist in time (to live), its configuration must evolve in such a way that provides easier access to the currents that flow through it.

This law has a simple basis. Dr. Bejan explains: "Everything that moves, whether animate or inanimate, is a flow system. All flow systems generate shape and structure in time in order to facilitate this movement across a landscape filled with resistance (for example, friction). Flows have two basic properties: the current that flows and the design through which it flows."[6]

Inventory movement is no different. The current (flow) of inventory is affected by the efficiency of flows across the supply chain's design. Supply chain systems must continually change over time, just like a river's structure changes as the volume of water flowing through it changes. Through such changes in its configuration, supply chains can provide greater access for the currents that flow through them. Inventory cannot move faster simply by willing it to do so; flow is clearly a function of how the system surrounding it is designed.

The physics constructal law is so simple, yet universal to many different phenomena. It governs any system and aligns with our observation that supply chains are indeed alive and unpredictable. This statement is also identified in other works. Lee Smolin, a theoretical physicist, wrote: "Life takes place in the context of a steady state far from an equilibrium situation with a steady flow of energy driving it, and within that context it's a semi-isolated system surrounded and protected by a membrane by which it controls the flow of material and energy across in each direction in order to promulgate its own survival and reproduction."[7]

Smolin's observation was often dismissed by physicists in the community because it was not testable. However, he dismissed this claim, and emphasized how time is NOW, not an illusion, and that we live in a relational world where reality consists only of what is real in each moment of time. This view of time is central to the ideas of supply chain physics: you are only as good as the inventory velocity of your supply chain today, and those are the only results that matter. The idea of real-time visibility is also aligned with the idea of reality consisting of what is happening right now, not yesterday or tomorrow. Or stated more simply, either the product was shipped on time to the customer's location today, or it wasn't! These moments of truth define the reality of time-bounded logistics performance, which suffered dramatically in 2020 and 2021.

Designing the Organization to Increase Supply Chain Velocity

Creating visibility is not enough by itself to drive velocity. Supply chain leaders need to define an operating environment that emphasizes increased velocity. In *The Physics of Life*, Dr. Bejan suggests that human existence itself is governed by physical flows.[8] We extend the idea of flows to consider how leaders should

structure their organizations to increase flow and promote velocity, which in turn can lead to increased customer satisfaction and
cash generation.

Tom Linton developed eight key questions that all supply
chain leaders should consider when designing their organization
for improved flow and greater immunity. These questions can
generate debate among a leadership team and hopefully lead to
action and changes in operating principles.[9] They can help to design the playbook that can lead to a more immune supply chain.
The fundamental tenet is that paying attention to the flow of
time vector is critical to a company's success. Business leaders
have only so many days in a year, and every action has a clock
attached to it. The following questions and guidelines can help
managers to design their supply chain ecosystems to promote
flow and reduce friction. They begin at a high level and move
down to more granular issues.

Question 1: Philosophy – What approach to supply chain fits your organization's industry, culture, time, technology, capabilities, and objectives?

The first question one should ponder is the degree of congru-
ence between your supply chain and the direction your business
is headed. In a football game, the offense and defense are alter-
nately represented by opposing teams. Within each team, players are assigned to either the offensive line or the defensive line.
Like a football coach, think about whether you are going to play
offense (expand your supply chains in new regions) or defense
(increase your company's disruption immunity).

Either way, aligning the supply chain to business objectives
involves considering how financial flows are being generated
and captured in the business model. Generating free cash flow is

becoming more important in a post-COVID era than the actual cost (e.g., low price) of goods in the supply chain. To this end, a strategy of incremental cost improvement may not be as important as increasing the velocity of movement of goods. Shareholders may also care more about velocity. Recent research has shown that a company's valuation is highly correlated with return on invested capital (ROIC),[10] and more companies are employing this metric in their capital budgeting. Another form used by retailers is gross margin return on inventory investment (GM-ROII).[11] Speed can contribute to share price growth by reducing inventory investments via faster shipment and by reducing lost revenue due to supply shortages. But cost of goods sold (COGS) also matters in this formula. Therefore, speed helps, but only to the degree that its positive impact on inventory and supply shortages is not exceeded by a negative impact on COGS.

At Flex, Tom Linton noted that he had more than 1,400 customers, 20,000 SKUs, 30 countries, 121 factories, 220,000 employees, and more than 1 million part numbers to manage in his supply chain. The company was drowning in complexity. He knew it was going to kill him unless he converted his role to become the "simplification officer," and he made it a goal to enhance the visibility of the supply chain.

On his first Monday in the office, he asked for a full report of all supply chain metrics, and his analyst told him he could get it done by Friday. Tom told him he needed it now, not in a week. So he set about creating a visibility platform that would provide an immediate understanding of what was happening in real time and allow him to quickly generate ideas to improve cash flow. But this took time – the team had to "defrag" the supply chain – and eventually he learned he had 59 days of inventory across his entire internal supply chain. He was able to compress this by four percent within one year.

How did this happen? Primarily by shining a light on all the inventory in the supply chain. By understanding where all the inventory was kept, the team identified all sorts of material sitting around. In many cases, it had been there for months or years. They disposed of inventory that was not moving. Further, they identified "planned lead times" within the planning system that had been input years ago and had not been updated. For instance, lead time for one category of goods was changed from four weeks to two weeks to reflect the true capability of suppliers and the system. As a result, "safety stock" and "reorder points" were reduced, and a lot of inventory was taken out of the channel. Every material flow was put to a simple test: Can I simplify this material flow as well as reduce material and lead time in the system? Doing so resulted in massive reductions in inventory within a year.

Here is the key concept behind these activities: Given unpredictable demand and supply, focus on improving cash flow (outside of price, which is set by the market) by condensing the distance between parties in the supply chain and/or increasing the velocity of materials and payments.

Assume products can be transported from China via ocean freight in 30 days or much faster by plane. Doing the latter costs more, but is that cost worth getting the goods earlier? To make this call, consider the tipping point, when flying goods from China is no longer cost effective. If one really wants to harness time as a competitive weapon, what needs to be done, and what are the relevant costs? These questions are particularly important in an era of global shifts in tariffs and trade laws, and managers need real-time data to render decisions that increase cash flow velocity. Much longer lead times for global sourcing and other disruptions will also drive changes in the way organizations re-design their supply chains.

Question 2: Policies – What rules are required to control organizational behavior within the legal and ethical boundaries established by management?

Policies are an important guide, even though employees often disregard them as bureaucratic. But policies can help drive the right behaviors, especially as they relate to quicker decision-making in the face of uncertainty.

At Flex, Tom Linton wrote the policies that would govern how the supply chain would run. To ensure that they were adhered to, he enabled a visibility platform called Flex Pulse. Nine rooms were set up around the globe, each with the equivalent of a large iPad on its wall. A data warehouse was created that pulled together data from 94 applications running data from across the Flex organization. This data was sent to the Pulse room, where the equivalent of a large iPad optimized it so that it could be viewed cohesively, applying some simple rules developed by management teams.

A simple policy that went along with the Pulse dashboard was that all inventory information was color-coded as yellow, green, or red. (See figure 2.1.) Managers were instructed to pay the most attention to the red parts of the dashboard. This is because, in general, 98 percent of supply chains (including Flex's) operate seamlessly without human intervention. For example, machines can adjust minimum order quantities if the lead time is reduced. The Pulse was designed to help employees deal with the two percent of issues that require human intervention, such as when a shift in trade positions may automatically divert shipments to different regions. Touchscreens in the Pulse rooms project several different visualizations to allow people to work together in real time on their mobile phones and help them understand what is happening and deal with situations as they arise.

FIGURE 2.1. *Flex's days of supply inventory map*

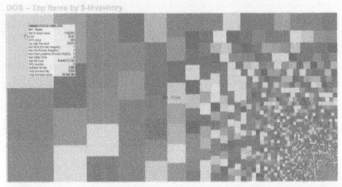

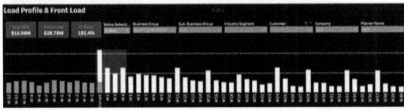

Question 3: Principles – What positions support a legal and ethical policy framework that will guide employees in the supply chain?

Defining the ethical behaviors that surround supply chain decisions is important from a regulatory perspective. Employees face the "moment of truth" when they are confronted with real-time data about the performance of their system. For instance, individuals may be forced to confront the fact that women and children are employed in tier-2 suppliers within their supply chain. Are they truly comfortable with this? Does this violate the terms of the International Labour Organization (ILO)? Would they want their own children working in a factory and not going to school? Visibility enables individuals to make decisions quickly, but the principles defining ethical behaviors ensure that they act ethically and do not cut corners. Ethical behavior also requires understanding the context and culture of the location of a firm's operating environment. Armed with this knowledge, individuals in the supply chain can ensure that a company's moral and ethical principles play out in their patterns of decision-making while complying with shifting local regulations.

Absolute principles are difficult to enforce in the real world, where they are open to interpretation and debate as well as political, cultural, and social norms. Corporate boards are often under fire for a variety of issues, and sustainability and human rights increasingly drive consumers to vote with their pocketbooks. Some of the many issues that undergo social and political debate include guns, use of military force, consumption of sugar, cigarettes, gambling, GMOs, fatty food – the list goes on! To find a common framework, it is important to establish an organizational policy tied to broadly accepted frameworks such as the ILO convention of the UN Global Compact. But these principles must also allow local flexibility. For instance, VF Corporation, a large apparel, footwear, and accessories company, reviews audits of factory conditions with suppliers in low-cost countries and helps them to meet the requirements of the ILO through coaching and training. At the same time, VF seeks to couch these standards in the context of the local cultural norms in places such as Vietnam, Bangladesh, and India. If a supplier still does not change and will not comply, VF will phase them out as a supplier. Acting locally is also important as global trade shifts in different directions, enabling businesses to react to local changes in regulations, culture, and people.

Question 4: Practices – How does your industry and company define its supply chain scope of practice?

A scope of practice refers to the boundaries within which decisions are made. The medical field describes a practice as the domain of a specific physician within which the physician is authorized to practice. An ear, nose, and throat physician, for example, might refer a patient to a physician with a different scope of practice, say, cardiology or pulmonology. Defining the scope of a practice determines the education requirements of medical students in that practice, the decisions over which a physician presides relative to other specialists, and the types of therapies and drugs physicians are allowed to prescribe.

Similarly, supply chain officers need to define their scope of practice according to the decisions in their domain and how their decisions interact with other functional business decisions. Talk to 10 supply chain officers, and each is likely to have a different scope of practice and different organizational relationships and governance with marketing, IT, finance, HR, etc. At Flex, Tom Linton's scope included the entire supply chain: procurement, transportation, warehouse management, customer order fulfillment, customer service, procure to pay, and trade relationships. This end-to-end governance allowed him to improve the integration of decision-making patterns across multiple activities in the supply chain.

While enviable, this scope of practice may not be appropriate for every company. Generally, supply chain officers with a broader scope of practice and more seniority have greater latitude to change the nature of decision-making and the contribution of the supply chain function to the overall business. The right level of governance between regional business decisions and globally centralized decisions must also be balanced. A policy that works well in the United States may not be appropriate in the context of Germany or China.

Question 5: Processes – How will your company carry out its philosophies, policies, and practices?

Many new supply chain officers begin their tenure by mapping out all the processes under their governance. This, they hope, will lead to automating processes, establishing tools for decision-making in the context of these processes, and making the processes more efficient. But all this could be a mistake. Jumping into improving current processes without first thinking about the previous four questions could improve or automate something that does not reflect the company's strategic direction. Is the current process already what you need, given what you want to achieve?

At Flex, the Pulse visualized the data and suppressed much of the noise around existing processes (see the top portion of figure 2.1). A simple chart depicted inventory, with the size indicative of the amount of cash tied up in that inventory. If the inventory was more than 60 days old the box was red; 30–60 days, yellow; and less than 30 days, green. These colored boxes were ordered from left to right by size, so managers could quickly focus on high-volume inventory that was not moving. This method prioritized action in real time. The takeaway is that giving people access to data that drives actions in real time is a game changer.

Visualization of supply chain data moves innovation from a concept to a process. Ideas become actions, not just great suggestions. Nowadays managers employ software and technology as part of the process used to make decisions, and acting on a graphical representation of events in a supply chain suddenly becomes meaningful. Red is bad; inventory is sitting around and not adding value. Attention needs to be focused on getting rid of the red and moving it to the green box or at least the yellow. This also drives accountability because executives can quickly look over a visualization and learn immediately how that area of practice is operating. However, leaders need to focus on their processes and the actions of their managers first and not worry about which particular software works best.

Question 6: Physics – What structural requirements define the places, facilities, and distances needed for efficient execution?

To improve flow and velocity, the physical characteristics of the supply chain will determine if flow is constricted or allowed to move in a natural fashion. This means consideration of the structural characteristics of the places, facilities, and distances between nodes to create effective customer value chains. Structural considerations include where facilities are located, where material is located, and how to avoid tying up cash. Managers need to design and optimize their business according to the physics of supply chains, because distance impacts time and money.

We live in a post-global world. Globalization is dying slowly because the economics of low-cost labor arbitrage has been turned on its head due to rising transportation costs. China has lifted more people out of poverty in the last 20 years than it did in the previous 5,000. Consumption is rising, and global politics are becoming tenser. A post-global world is actually good for supply chains because organizations will seek to manufacture locally and resources will be driven closer to customers and suppliers.

Yet most supply chains are rarely organized simply. Flex employed a tool called SimFlex, a supply chain simulator that allowed analysts to look at the company's network design. At a high level, Flex's supply chain looked exceedingly complex, like a bowl of spaghetti. SimFlex allowed executives to visualize the long distances between nodes, the volume of needless back-and-forth trips occurring between locations, and the nodes where inventory was sitting still. This visualization left the transformation team with the impression that Flex's supply chain was entirely random in design, even though executives had spent years planning it and making it better. Ultimately, simulation tools can draw attention to flows that may be obscured.

The physics of flow is a function of distance and time, and many supply chains have emerged as long and slow due to the evolution of global sourcing over the last forty years. The changing nature of global trade patterns and the consideration of increased localization of supply chains despite apparently higher costs may lead to rethinking the structure of physical supply chains. This is not just a passing trend.[12] Experts predict that localization of supply chains, or nearshoring, and technological advancements that level the playing field between the United States and countries with lower labor costs will emerge in the coming years. The US government has also introduced bills to onshore medical supplies, and Rob Handfield testified before a Senate Committee in May 2021 on the idea of building a more immune domestic supply chain to become more self-reliant.[13]

Question 7: People – What skills are required to support the company's mission?

This question raises several others to consider regarding the people in the organization. Are hiring, training and retention methods working well? Are people being trained to think critically about supply chain data, and leverage the insights they get from the data? The popular press is replete with predictions that human problem-solving can be improved by machines, but that is not the whole story. For instance, a computer algorithm may be able to suggest the optimal location to build warehouses, but ultimately human judgment is required. Do these locations make sense based on the locations of multiple other nodes in the network? While machines are good at automating rote tasks, which account for about 80 percent of all supply chain tasks, human beings are needed to ultimately make decisions and manage exceptions – and there will always be exceptions. A machine can likely reset a minimum order quantity when lead times drop. Similarly, payment processes can be automated. But human beings will always need to execute tasks involving more subtle indicators and judgments. And for some tasks like packaging products into boxes at an Amazon facility, humans still function much better than robots!

One of the most important components of change that will accompany the move to a post-COVID economy is the need for critical thinking. It is likely that more people will work from home and will make decisions jointly based on perceptions and debate involving the use of data. Critical thinking is the ability to combine data/statistical/information literacy with analysis, interpretation, and evaluation to support organizational data-driven decision-making (DDDM).

Organizations of all sizes, both for-profit and not-for-profit, are working to improve their employees' critical-thinking capabilities. Critical thinking is a common term, yet there is no generally accepted definition for it. Strong and continually expanding critical-thinking skills are required for data-driven decision-making and problem-solving skills that enable a company to exploit machine-based learning for decision velocity and flow. One definition and set of attributes that proves useful is the following:

Critical thinking is a manner of thinking that employs curiosity, creativity, skepticism, analysis, and logic, where[14]

- Curiosity is a desire to learn.
- Creativity involves viewing information from multiple perspectives.

- Skepticism embodies a "trust but verify" mindset.
- Analysis is systematically examining and evaluating evidence.
- Logic means reaching well-founded conclusions.

While some people have a natural aptitude in these areas, everyone can learn and/or enhance their capabilities. Development of critical-thinking skills is a foundation for effective processing of real-time data interpretation and data analysis. Increased training and mentoring is needed to help new managers understand how to engage with real-time data, probe deeper into the data for insights, connect disparate facts, and develop logical conclusions that lead to effective actions. This capability is not easily taught. It requires practice and a willingness to allow individuals to fail as they learn. Humans' ability to consume large volumes of data, use graphical visualization and statistical analysis to recognize relationships among key variables, and complement these insights with other data through exploration and interaction with technology will become extremely important. Critical thinking can produce the advanced insights that lead to effective supply chain immunity and improved flow.

Question 8: Performance – What types of objectives indicate success? Are they supported through agile decision-making?

Timely and functionally aligned business objectives must be emphasized through performance indicators and improvement targets that keep everyone pointed in the same direction. The most common indicators are revenue targets, income statement profitability, and balance sheet metrics; other indicators follow from these targets to individual lines of business and functions. But decision-making agility is rarely measured, even though it is one of the most important indicators of supply chain immunity. Agile decision-making is generally a function of effective critical thinking.

Research suggests that more agile companies rely less on top-down, command-and-control decision-making.[15] Agility, sometimes referred to as situational intelligence, can be defined as the ability of individuals to rapidly consume real-time data, assess what is going on around them, and quickly make a good (but not always perfect) decision. A 2017 McKinsey survey showed that agile units performed significantly better than those that were not agile, but relatively few were acting in a truly agile manner.[16] The COVID pandemic required people to work from home and to self-organize into agile teams mandated to make more day-to-day decisions. These agile teams relied on data and analytics to make decisions much more quickly through aligned and consensual decision-making. Organizations that were successful made agile teams both accountable and flexible by ensuring that the right subject matter experts were assigned to the right teams.[17]

Here again, the natural world provides a wonderful metaphor for demonstrating the power of agility. When driving from Asheville to Raleigh, North Carolina, Tom Linton observed a flock of starlings murmuring; the birds were flying in a cohesive pattern, guided by some sixth sense involving intense collaboration among thousands of individual birds in motion. Experts in bird migration also noted that a massive group of golden-winged warblers had suddenly flown from Eastern Tennessee to Florida. This happened two days before a massive hurricane went through the region. What was the data that prompted this agile decision on the part of warblers to be alerted to the hurricane two days before it arrived? Experts believe the warblers sensed the incoming storm, while it was still over the Gulf of Mexico, through low-frequency sound waves (infrasound) that storms make.

But what does this mean for supply chain agility? Managers also need to use signals to better predict what disruptive events might be on the horizon this afternoon, next week, or next month in supply chain channels. How can agile teams better understand what is ahead by leveraging data produced by artificial intelligence and enhanced cognitive thinking? What national healthcare systems are needed to help countries to mitigate the effects of global disruptions such as pandemics? Technologies may one day be able to sense these shifts for us, but we need humans with agile and critical thinking skills who can pick up on these signals and know what to do with them.

The following two General Motors (GM) case studies provide insight into how these eight questions can be addressed in practice to create greater responsiveness, agility, and supply chain immunity. After the 2008 financial crisis, GM pursued a low-cost supply chain as a conscious business strategy.[18] GM was not the only company to do so; there was a massive movement in almost every industry to outsource to low-cost suppliers worldwide. However, in response to the 2011 earthquake and tsunami in Japan, GM completely shifted its operating model to design a more immune supply chain better prepared to deal with global disasters. This move illustrates the importance of velocity when it comes to acting quickly to avert shutting down the business and contributing to national shortages of critical equipment during a pandemic.

Case Study 1: The Impact of Japan's Tsunami on GM's Supply Network (2011)

On March 11, 2011, a magnitude-9 earthquake shook northeastern Japan, unleashing a savage tsunami.[19] The effects of the underwater earthquake were felt around the world, from

Norway's fjords to Antarctica's ice sheet.[20] The tsunami caused a cooling system failure at the Fukushima Daiichi Nuclear Power Plant, which resulted in a level-7 nuclear meltdown and release of radioactive materials.[21] The electrical power and backup generators were overwhelmed by the tsunami, and the plant lost its cooling capabilities.

Several tier-1 suppliers provided GM components from suppliers located all over the world, and many of these were located in Southeast Asia and China. After studying their bill of materials immediately following the earthquake on March 11, the GM response team believed that only 25 Japanese suppliers had been affected. Three days later, after forming a risk-mitigation team, managers realized that more than 390 suppliers would be affected. This would potentially shut down all North American and European plants in the next week, with all remaining plants shut down by the end of March. But then the disruption continued to ripple throughout the supply base. By March 24, the team had identified 1,551 GM suppliers that would be shut down, and every single one of GM's 16 global facilities would be affected until the end of April.

The reason for the contagion was that many GM suppliers relied on electronic chips and semiconductors produced by the same set of tier-2 suppliers that had been caught in the Japanese earthquake. Even though GM had redundancy in the tier-1 supply base, all of the tier-1 suppliers sourced from the *same* tier-2 Japanese suppliers. By March 29, more than 1,800 suppliers were affected; by April 13, the team realized that a staggering 5,329 suppliers could not produce GM parts across 110 category groups.

The response team recognized that they needed to document these shortages, and they developed a technique called a white space chart, which assessed the number of days until each facility was shut down. The white space chart was essentially a visual dashboard to show at a glance which vehicle platforms and parts were affected, when critical parts would run out, and when new or alternative parts might show up. It also showed when each one of GM's 16 assembly plants might be shut down due to a lack of parts.[22] These white board charts spanned an entire room. A triangle indicated a potential problem, and an X marked a definite disruption to production. The timeline stretched out almost a year on the right-hand side of the chart. The timeline also showed when GM expected to restart production using one of three stop-gap activities: (a) recovery of the original supplier, (b) bringing alternative suppliers on line, or (c) finding an engineering work-around.

This approach to consolidating data into a centralized location, combined with daily calls to suppliers and plants, helped to close the white space facility by facility. By mid-April, five facilities were back up to 100 percent production. By May 27, of GM's 16 plants, 13 were up to 100 percent production. This occurred because GM was able to quickly get access to data, allowing the company to respond to and manage issues one by one, working with suppliers, finding parts, managing inventory, and dealing with regional issues.

Case Study 2: Scaling Up Ventilator Supply Chains in a Time of COVID (2020)[23]

Used as a verb, scale refers to the ability to grow or expand in a proportional and usually profitable way. Used as a noun, it means proportional growth, especially of production or profit. Scaling up a business is a capability that we believe is critical to establish greater supply chain immunity and is consistent with improving flow. This case study reiterates another lesson learned by GM in improving supply chain immunity and illustrates the critical steps required in recognizing a problem exists, defining the solution, and scaling up to deploy it.

In early March 2020, the world was beginning to recognize the impact that COVID was going to have on communities all over the United States, Canada, and Mexico. A nonprofit organization connected GM with Ventec, an established company based in Bothell, Washington, that produces a multi-function ventilator, the VOCSN.[24] At the time, there was a growing concern about the lack of ventilators, particularly in states such as New York, New Jersey, and Michigan. GM was exploring ways that the company could help with the COVID cause.

GM and Ventec quickly confirmed that they wanted to work together to help the United States and the world manage the massive influx of ICU patients, who required ventilators to survive. Specifically, GM offered to help Ventec to increase its limited production capacity of VOCSN ventilators. The goal was to ramp up ventilator manufacturing capabilities by having GM set up its own manufacturing facility to produce ventilators. The plan was to use parts from Ventec's existing supply base and new GM suppliers that were being tooled up to support the increased volume. This had to be done under extremely compressed time requirements. The motto for this effort became "One Team – One Mission – One Month." Working as one unified team, GM and Ventec worked to achieve a one-focus mission: to produce ventilators at a scale that was required to meet demand, and to produce the first ventilator one month after the start date.

Ryan Arens has worked at GM for 20 years. After spending the first part of his career in engineering, he began working on several program launches that eventually migrated him to the world of purchasing. He was notified of his assignment as the project lead for the effort within the purchasing and supply chain organization to support the coordination of activities between GM and Ventec.

Ryan recalls how quickly things moved once the decision was made to proceed with ventilator production. "We created a start-up company structure within the purchasing and supply chain organization to get the activity moving, knowing that it could be much more nimble, and this allowed us to go very fast. We went from the first discussions with Ventec, led by Phil Kienle, VP of Manufacturing at GM, to the first product going out the door in a month."

Individuals at GM and the company's suppliers worked 24/7 to achieve this goal. It started with a discussion, and then on March 19 the GM team members flew to Bothell to meet with Ventec to understand how to physically produce the unit. By the next morning, purchasing pulled together a team to organize supply chain components. GM team members went onsite at Ventec to study part drawings and determine how to source components. They then began to transfer production designs to GM's own suppliers for more than 500 unique parts, and plans were put in place to prepare GM's factory in Kokomo, Indiana, to begin production of ventilators.

GM was able to contact some of Ventec's existing suppliers to source parts within days and have those parts shipped to plants in two weeks. Fortunately, GM's supply base was agile and willing to help. GM's culture to pitch in made all the difference in scaling up and acting quickly.

Summary: A Supply Chain Immunity Playbook

The first case study illustrates how GM managed the white space in its supply chain during a global disaster, the Japanese tsunami, given the challenges of different time zones, languages, and cultures. The second case study shows how GM was able to rapidly scale up production in one month beginning on March 19, 2020, and on April 17, 2020 was able to deliver the first ventilator to a Chicago hospital. This led to thousands of ventilators being produced. Both case studies provide some important lessons for readers to consider.

- **Create indicators that provide early warning signals of both short-term problems and longer-term potential disruptions, and establish a governance structure for acting on these signals.** For instance, one GM executive we interviewed said: "One of the big lessons learned coming out of the tsunami involved learning how to separate day-to-day firefighting from long-term risk decisions. What are the yellow flags that tell you something is impending? For example, one of the big key performance indicators (KPIs) I monitored as a yellow flag was premium freight, and how much of it was going by ground versus air. If I started to see a lot going by air, this alerted me immediately that something was not right. The supplier was running over their stated capacity, the schedule was being changed on short notice, or we may have had a production issue. Every morning, I would review what the air charges were for that day: What was it for, and how much? This was a great risk indicator for problems that were occurring in the supply chain, and frequently led to a phone call and discussion."

- **Standardize parts, components, and SKUs to create supply flexibility.** Prior to 2011, GM exposed itself to greater disruption risk by designing a large number of parts with a lot of variation, which in turn resulted in a lot of single-source components. By reducing complexity and the number of unique parts, especially across vehicle platforms, parts can be shared between platforms when there is a disruption. Moreover, the volume can be spread across more suppliers, which reduces supply risk during a disruption.

- **Build deep knowledge of supplier and logistics capacity in a global supply chain.** A GM leader explained: "Bo Andersson [GM's Chief Procurement Officer] wanted every purchase category team to have at least one global supplier as a result of the pressure felt from 2008, so we all went to China or Malaysia. This became very much a 'check-the-box' exercise, and we often used overseas suppliers without doing the right level of due diligence. This came back to bite us later as our volume went up significantly in 2010, and many of these suppliers did not have the capacity to meet our demand because we hadn't audited their manufacturing capacity levels. In addition, our logistics costs went through the roof as we were now air expressing parts from Malaysia and China to GM's four assembly plants in Mexico (Teluca, Saltillo, and others)."

- **Invest in real-time event-tracking technologies with a dedicated response team.** Since the tsunami, GM has invested heavily in risk-monitoring technologies, including Resilinc. Bill Hurles, GM's executive director of supply chain, noted: "In 2011, our white space charts involved a lot of manual data tracking. But it taught us that to manage risk, we needed to become more aggressive in collecting data on the supply base and communicating risk to everyone in the company. You don't want to be a 'chicken little' and imagine the sky is falling over every single little event. But there needs to be at least a conversation on what is the issue, what are we doing, and what more can we do to create an immune supply chain?" In addition, GM has automated the tracking of parts all over the world, and it is alerted instantaneously when a disruption occurs in the network. "You only need a single part shortage on a vehicle to stop a production line – and there are 30,000 parts on an automobile. An entire automotive production line can shut down for lack of a five-cent lug nut."

- **Weigh the cost of not investing when considering allocation of resources for supply chain immunity**. Particularly in a post-COVID world, quantifying risk and embracing identification of supply chain risks has become more vital than ever. Visibility into the supply chain can help executives understand where their network has the potential to shut down their business. Purchasing executives tend to only consider the volume of spend as the key driver for risk; however, any single component or service can potentially be the fatal chink in the armor. All parts are equal when it comes to supply chain risk. For instance, an automotive facility of 3,000 highly paid workers is a significant cost that can add up to $1 million for every minute of downtime.

- **Employ a flattened leadership structure to rapidly scale up a disaster response**. During the Ventec scale-up, GM pulled together functional leads within purchasing and supply chain, who then operated within their team and supported team members in their own area. There were communication calls every day with the team to ensure clarity of updates, share information on run rates, and communicate with suppliers.

- **Prioritize sourcing plans based on criticality**. GM classified components into different categories to drive their sourcing strategy as follows: (a) "super-critical A+" components meant using a known, existing supplier from Ventec's supply-base; (b) "A" parts, considered critical to design, involved using either an incumbent Ventec supplier or, if they had scale or capacity constraints, a GM supplier; and (c) "B and C" parts, for which Ventec gave the OK for GM to pick a new supplier and source those parts. Communication of electronic design blueprints initially occurred through email attachments with suppliers to ensure rapid responses. Determination of critical parts and suppliers enabled prioritization of work to ensure the scale-up of part design and manufacturability.

- **Leverage scale to support critical suppliers on tier-2 sourcing.** After both these incidents, GM mapped its supply base down to tier 2 and tier 3, and today it can move parts around the world quite easily. During the Ventec scale-up, GM was able to help its tier-1 suppliers with components that they had difficulty sourcing. These included circuit boards, chips, sensors, consumables (hoses, etc.), and ventilator motors where there were long lead times and capacity constraints worldwide. During COVID, many other manufacturers were chasing these same parts, and many Asian suppliers were also shut down because of COVID. Because of its size and scale, GM could assist its suppliers in their efforts to influence tier-2 suppliers to support them.
- **Simplify contracting and negotiation to improve immunity.** During the Ventec scale-up, GM eliminated lengthy negotiations over tooling costs and simplified contract terms. The company simply informed Ventec suppliers that it wanted to use the same price that Ventec had contracted with them. Ventec's part qualification process and network were adopted at GM's facility. Automotive companies generally manage quality at the supplier's site to ensure that good material comes out of the supplier's facility before it reaches the automotive company's plant. GM tested quality at its facility and the supplier's site. More expensive additive manufacturing was used to speed up the timing of production to get tooling in place.
- **Ensure safety of all critical workers throughout the end-to-end supply chain.** During the Ventec process, GM implemented COVID safety protocols across its supply base,

including how to enter and exit a building, to avoid any part of the supply chain shutting down as well as to keep people safe. Health and safety of all personnel are instrumental to the continuity of the supply chain. In addition, it is critical that everyone knows how important they are in the network.

Simplification of supply chain flows is a concept that has many important implications for how we design the supply chains of the future. In particular, the trade wars and COVID restrictions that brought supply chains to their knees are causing individuals to rethink the importance of flow. One way that the concept of flow manifests itself is in the field of thermodynamics, which we apply to the trends in global trade flows that occurred in 2020. We explore this concept in the next chapter. Specifically, we will extend the idea of physical flows to the flow of global trade. The implications, as you will see, are significant. We believe they point to some important changes in the global economy and how individuals will operate in their jobs.

CHAPTER THREE

Thermodynamics and Evolutionary Flow

Locusts have no King
Yet they all march forth in formation

Proverbs 30:27 (Likely by King Solomon 600 BCE)

The observation that animates me is that where most people see confusion and randomness and complexity – the minority sees a pattern and a purpose and direction. There is a constant evolutionary design that is unstoppable and at work in the supply chain.

Adrian Bejan, Duke University, interview, April 20, 2020

In the last three years (2019–22), political and health events have threatened supply chain models of globalization. The recent separation of the United Kingdom through Brexit, and the tariffs imposed by the Trump administration against China, set a backdrop for increasing isolationist policies and moving away from globalized supply chains. The rapid spread of the COVID virus shut down every industry in every country in the world, escalating calls by lawmakers to reshore manufacturing to avoid future disruptions to healthcare systems and economic stability.

The media is rife with suggestions that we are edging toward a new era in which supply chain disruptions and tariffs threaten global trade, and we will return to becoming isolated islands of commerce. The common theme is that organizations have sought the lowest-cost supply sources, and Western executives should begin moving manufacturing from China to the United States, the European Union, and South America.[1]

But does this shift make sense? Our discussions with executives suggest that committing to outsourcing in low-cost countries requires a minimum planning horizon of five years because the shift requires supplier qualification, audits, start-up costs, quality certification, and ongoing ramp-up. Other discussions reveal that certain supply chains are embedded in Asia, and the statement that "outsourced jobs will never return to Western countries" is being heard still. Executives need some guidance to help them think through this confusing array of options. Yet, our central belief is that there is order within the chaos if one looks more carefully, and that the order of events follows a structured flow that is perhaps imperceptible to most.

On the topic of reshoring, we tend to agree with the notion that localization of all supply chains is unlikely. Localization will depend on how embedded suppliers are and the relative mobility of suppliers to co-locate in the countries where their customers are. It will not always be practical for suppliers to move. For example, consider that 80 percent of the world's production of automotive brake pads are produced by four manufacturers in Shandong Province, China. To establish alternative sources that are competitive, qualified, and capable of scaling production levels would cost much more than the 25 percent tariffs that many companies pay today to import from China. An implicit assumption behind much of the hype in the press is that COVID caught everyone by surprise, and that executives who foolishly ignored the risks of outsourcing to China for years are now paying the price. Pundits further posit that in their pursuit of low-cost production, global corporations naively assumed that nothing could disrupt their supply chains. Government-imposed tariffs were simply a passing political inconvenience; Brexit restrictions would eventually be negotiated away with Brussels.

In this chapter, we offer an alternative viewpoint that follows from the observations in the previous chapter: namely, that the shift in globalization toward localization is part of a natural evolution of supply chains that unfolds over time in a predictable fashion. We will provide examples that show how this shift has occurred over the past few years and continues to unfold today. Before we do that, we need to refer to an important law of thermodynamics found in physics.

The Constructal Law

In chapter 2, we explored how the constructal law of physics accounts for the phenomenon of evolution. It dictates the configuration, form, and design of both animate and inanimate flow systems and how they evolve in ways that provide easier access to the currents that flow through them.

The constructal law describes the arrow of time (i.e., the direction of the evolution of flow over a period of time). It is part of the field of thermodynamics, which "owes its immense power – its utmost generality – to the fact that its laws apply to *any* imaginable system," Bejan writes. "At bottom, thermodynamics is a *discipline*. It has precise rules, words, and laws. Any analysis, any discussion, must begin with defining the system unambiguously, and sticking with it."[2]

So let us return to our argument that supply chains flow like other physical phenomena in nature. The most obvious example is how supplier networks generally evolve to the point of lowest total cost. This is a natural progression, as defined by the exchange of goods and services between enterprises that are shaped by trade flows.

An example from the natural world illustrates this idea. When water flowing in a river encounters a barrier, such as a sandbar, stones, or a shift in elevation, the flow of water is redirected to a new path. The flow of water seeks to find the path of least resistance, and over time the river may adopt a completely different route over the surface of the earth. We believe that this is happening today with supply chains: as new obstacles appear, supply chain flows are being redirected to a path that presents the fewest obstacles.

How do supply chains evolve? A company's supply chain design is integral to its competitive footprint. This design is not static, and it is influenced by the decisions managers make when confronted by major disruptions such as trade wars, tariffs, or global pandemics such as COVID. Various forces act on supply chain designs, which then evolve in a balanced manner that improves the flow of the entire system.[3] To summarize: supply chains evolve freely through forces of change in a predictable fashion, and evolve to a position of lowest total cost. Let us examine this with an example: Brexit.

Brexit

In mid-2016, the United Kingdom voted to leave the European Union (EU) by a majority of 51 percent to 49 percent. Following the vote, UK Prime Minister David Cameron resigned and the Financial Times Stock Exchange (FTSE) 250 index fell by 13 percent. The value of the pound sterling dropped 10 percent versus the euro and remained 12 percent lower in the three years that followed. On March 29, 2017, Theresa May, the new UK prime minister, triggered Article 50, giving the United Kingdom two years to ratify an exit deal with the EU member states. Theresa May agreed to two trade deals with the EU over the next two years, but each deal was subsequently rejected by the UK parliament. The initial exit date of March 31, 2019, passed with no agreement, and the date of departure was pushed back to October 31, 2019. Having failed to ratify the deal with the UK parliament, Theresa May resigned her post on June 7, 2019.

Boris Johnson came to power on July 24, 2019, and moved quickly to reach a new agreement with the EU. His deal was put to parliament, but it did not pass the meaningful vote by the required date of October 31, 2019. The Brexit date was subsequently pushed back to January 31, 2020, and Boris Johnson called a snap election, which he won convincingly. With his new parliament in place, MPs voted on Boris Johnson's deal to depart the EU on January 31, 2020, and it passed by a significant margin. Since then, the United Kingdom has been in transition as it attempts to reach a comprehensive trade agreement for goods and services with the EU.

Brexit was a disruption that clearly affected many industries in the United Kingdom and Europe, re-shaping the trade flows that existed prior to its passing. But because it happened so slowly and was drawn out over such a long period of time, organizations were able to change their flows in such a way that they could hedge their bets and come up with solutions. One manager working for an aerospace manufacturing firm in the United Kingdom whom we interviewed explained that his company's supply chain design is centralized and entrenched. Due to the long life span of its final product, the company is locked into suppliers who provide components and spare parts while the product is in service: "Our supply chain is quite entrenched because once the contract is awarded, the supply contract is for the life of the product, which could easily be for 15 years," he said.

He explained that the supply chain design is influenced by a number of pressures applied by the UK and EU governments. These are in the forms of regulations and funding as well as social pressures related to anticipated restrictions to the free movement of labor following Brexit.

"I have worked with French, Italians, Germans, all within the UK, and I have been able to travel freely between all of our customers' different sites," he continued. "When you start putting those barriers in, it starts to impact the ability to do business face to face. Also, foreign colleagues are going home because of the uncertainty of Brexit and the xenophobia that appeared almost overnight."

This quote suggests that Brexit is exerting social pressures on the supply chain that are having an impact on human flows. European employees are returning home because of uncertainty surrounding their ability to live and work in the United Kingdom and also in response to perceptions of prejudice. Impeding the flow of people moving between countries in Europe, as well as changing the trade flows, is having a significant impact on how companies in the United Kingdom and Europe do business.

One might think this is too general an example. However, the shift occurs like a river, often in such slow increments that it is not noticeable over time. Every supply chain shifts to adapt to its ecosystem, but the supply chain shifts have rarely been compared to the idea of evolutionary design. This pattern does not show up until one steps back and looks at the big picture of evolutionary flows. Most supply chain managers do not notice this shift because they tend to be iterative and focused on transactions, often tweaking and making small and subtle changes to their supply chains. Managers often seek to optimize short-term costs or negotiate better pricing with suppliers.

In the current environment, however, such activities have proven to be of little consequence compared to the massive forces of economic disruption over the last three years. In the face of significant shifts in the ecosystem brought about by the pressure of globalization and COVID, doing the same thing over and over hoping it will improve the situation is a death sentence. It is part of the supply chain manager's disposition to focus on a negotiated cost savings of five percent to 10 percent for logistics or on the purchase price while failing to see the challenges of the bigger changes around them. Such savings do not amount to much when six months' worth of orders is wiped off the books by a COVID virus or a Brexit event, or when a trade deal increases tariffs by 25 percent. One executive we spoke with noted that "procurement people are too slow to see what is happening around them, and today are failing to see how digital technologies are changing the rules of the game for competition."

How have the last three years of tariffs, trade wars, Brexit, and COVID changed our supply chain ecosystem? Perhaps we need to think of them as a natural progression of events that follow the movement to low-cost country sourcing, which increased rapidly over the last 20 years. In this light, COVID signifies a tipping point triggered in 2016 with the beginning of the Trump and Brexit era. The reaction of the Trump administration to global sourcing is a direct outcome of the dissatisfaction of his base, many of whom had their jobs displaced to China. One might argue that Brexit was a function of the anxiety by some of the UK population about immigration levels. Regardless of the political factors at play, these events are the tip of the iceberg, following a trend toward economic and political dissociation between the East and West. Likewise, many maintain COVID was a freak event, but we are reminded that it was also a simple evolution of the flu, meaning pandemics might recur.[4] Perhaps all of these events are not coincidental at all, but are predictable in the context of the natural flow of global commerce.

In hindsight, several examples point to this predictability of events. First, consumers have become much more aware of where their products are manufactured and the human labor conditions in which they are produced. The passing of Modern Slavery Acts by Australia, the United Kingdom, and California, supported by increasing calls for greater transparency facilitated by mobile technology and cloud-based capabilities, are driving organizations to be more accountable about the activities that lie buried deep inside their supply chains. Organizations are no longer able to hide their tier-2 and tier-3 suppliers from view, as NGOs are going in and taking photographs of what is happening in these factories. Transparency and visibility are making people aware that all is not right in factories where cheap apparel and electronics are produced with forced, migrant, and child labor. This will also likely change the way that production occurs in low-cost countries.

Second, disruptions at the US and Chinese ports exposed the fragility of global logistics, and how dependent we are on products made overseas. During the pandemic, one manager at the Strategic National Stockpile noted that "I had no idea that 90% of our healthcare products were all produced in China and Asia!" This has launched a call to reshore many of these healthcare products, yet most hospitals are unwilling to pay the higher prices for domestically produced N95 masks (for instance). A third example involves the calls by governments to reshore semiconductor manufacturing, a response to the massive shortages facing almost every industry today. The naïve assumption behind these calls for reshoring is that we can build a semiconductor fabrication plant in Arizona and be independent. However, semiconductor manu-facturing is a highly complex science! Taiwan Semiconductor has more than 2,500 tier 1 suppliers, and more than 10,000 tier 2 sup-pliers. A fab plant can take upwards of three to five years to build! The public calls for reshoring to America are clearly unaware of the complexity of changing supply chain flows.

In retrospect, then, were the trade wars, Brexit, and the global pandemic destined to happen? We think so. The fall-out from many of the past years' trade wars, coupled with the massive impact of the coronavirus, has permanently reshaped the way global companies do business. This evolution has been much more rapid than in the past. The move toward localization of global supply bases is already underway, spurred on by political events.[5] But as we point out, it won't happen overnight, just as a river's flow takes time to shift. Pre-pandemic, there was already a rising concern around supply chain risks. A decade ago, many companies felt comfortable as suppliers consolidated and cen-tralized, often solely in China. But then they began to lose faith in globalization and made plans to onshore. Rising tensions in the South China Sea and heightened technology-theft concerns played a role in mood change, as did the Trump administration's broad use of tariffs and verbal warnings.

There is a direct relationship between supply chains that evolve through change and executives who seek to innovate. When confronted by significant barriers such as a global epi-demic, executives will convene and find intelligent alternatives. There may be short-term suffering and economic displacement. Factories will shut down, customers will cancel orders, revenue may drop, and share prices may plummet. Before the coronavi-rus hit, many apparel manufacturers had already pulled out of China but were still reliant on intermediate goods that can shut down their supply chains.[6]

Here is an example. The garment industry, which is less cap-
ital-intensive and easier to move, was among the first to break
out of China. Companies looking for low-cost labor moved production to places such as Bangladesh, one of the world's largest
clothing exporters after China. But intermediate goods will also
likely move out of China, especially healthcare products, which
were unavailable during COVID. Rob Handfield spoke at a Senate committee hearing on legislation that is looking at reshoring
active pharmaceutical ingredients and other critical pharmaceutical product inputs from India back to the United States.[7] These
are natural occurrences that accompany change, and creative
forces are triggered by such discontinuities in supply. Because
global change is inevitable, evolutionary design is required to
adapt to the shifts that occur in supply chain ecosystems. One
might see this as politicians weaponizing trade through tariffs
designed to punish countries that are not opening borders. But
what we might be observing instead is a natural shift toward
supply chain designs that are a function of political, economic,
and social sentiments.

Innovation seeks to rethink the way that decisions are made
and to dynamically update how supply chains operate. Evolutionary design requires that individuals constantly scan the
environment for emerging patterns or changes in how material
moves through their supply chains. Both are required to adapt to
changes in our global economy.

Forecasting Supply Chain Evolutionary Design

Flows represent tendencies that are predictable and are part of a
process called "organization." Let us return to our river example.
As a river flows it forms channels over time, and these broader

channels are positioned to stay in place for perpetuity, based on a hierarchy of smaller channels that flow in harmony with the large channel. Scientific principles dictate that roughly three to five tributaries feed into a larger channel.[8] The birth and life of a river basin continues to change over time. When rain falls uniformly over time in a green area, it gouges a groove or channel in the earth that collects the water and which, over time, allows water to flow more easily. The rainwater flows in a particular direction. The directed flow is an evolutionary pattern that over the long term dictates how the river basin will develop. For a flow system to continue to exist, it will evolve in such a way that it provides greater access to the natural movement of the river's current. All matter flows toward an end state, whether it is the lowest gravitational pull or the natural pull of wind and geography.

This also applies to humans and animals; those that morph to move more easily on the landscape will survive. Over time, humans have increased the speed at which they can move across land, aided by engineering, the discovery of the heat engine, the energy plants that feed our power outlets, and the evolution of humans operating machines. The development of the internal combustion engine converted heat from fuel into work and dumped the remainder into the ambient environment. The science of energy, a discipline called thermodynamics, focuses on how to squeeze more work from every unit of fuel consumed, and it is this law that is relevant to our discussion.

From a thermodynamics perspective, "work" describes the act of using fuel or energy to cause movement. Work is dissipated when any mass is moved, because movement requires the burning of fuel. People move based on the design of their bodies, wind moves in reaction to air temperature and pressure, and water moves in reaction to gravitational pull and the channels through which it flows. Geologists can examine the makeup of soil and the design of water flows in a certain area and can envision when future flows will likely occur.

Now let us think about predicting the movement in something designed by human beings: the Atlanta airport. This is a great example of designing for flow. The facility is designed to move people to various locations in the airport structure as quickly as possible. The dimensions of the facility are smaller for movement of flow that is slower, such as where people walk between gates in the same terminal. But the facility also identifies where flow needs to be fast, specifically the underground subway that transports people between terminals. The architect's natural rule of design was summarized by the guideline that "the time to go short and slow (between gates) is the same as the time to go long and fast (between terminals)." This period is five minutes anywhere in the Atlanta terminal.[9] The law of thermodynamics predicts how flows of travelers will function during normal operating conditions in the Atlanta airport.

But can the natural flows of supply chains be predicted using the same principles of thermodynamics? We have already discussed how supply chains throw off more cash when they move material faster. The constructal law suggests that executives and supply chain planners can envision how their supply chain flows will evolve. Granted, such flow predictions will be less scientific than a physicist's, and less accurate and precise. However, we can begin to project what this natural evolution will look like for supply chains of the future based on the flows we have witnessed to date.

Our first prediction is that supply chains of the future will evolve toward congregated, localized enterprises based on the forces of compression. This is not an earth-shattering notion. In the early twentieth century, Alfred Marshall[10] studied the "localisation of industry" effect of networks. He found that a consistent number of specialized firms form a local system of production in which the production chain is divided into several phases distributed over a cluster of independent companies. When companies in similar industries are located close to one another, such positive results as knowledge-sharing among common supply bases emerge, and a concentrated, skilled labor pool can emerge. The flows of tacit knowledge sharing are much more easily facilitated in a community of localized organizations. The same applies to the application of emerging technology such as additive manufacturing, as a case in Australia illustrated where small companies in a community all jointly benefited from innovative discoveries on how to exploit the technology to advantage.[11]

In another example, automotive companies who co-located in Detroit were able to reap multiple benefits. Michael Porter, in his book on competitive strategy, wrote about the increasing pace of productivity, innovation, and business formation in clusters.[12] In the last 20 years, the focus has increased on knowledge-intensive clusters such as Silicon Valley, a distinct form of value network characterized by geographical proximity among firms operating within it. Others have emerged, including pharmaceutical clusters in Research Triangle Park, North Carolina; high-tech clusters in Washington, DC; and increasingly, additive manufacturing clusters in Ohio and Australia. One of the largest clusters of automotive production in the world is not in Detroit but in Saltillo, Mexico, due to the lower labor costs and flexible export treaties.

Shifting industries from one country to another in response to a government regulation or tariff does not occur overnight. The process of shifting an industry to a local cluster takes time and often takes massive investment. In light of current events, executives are certainly beginning to consider such investments because the supply shortages brought about by COVID are forcing them to rethink whether cost leadership still justifies

FIGURE 3.1. *Wage rates across China, Mexico, and Vietnam*

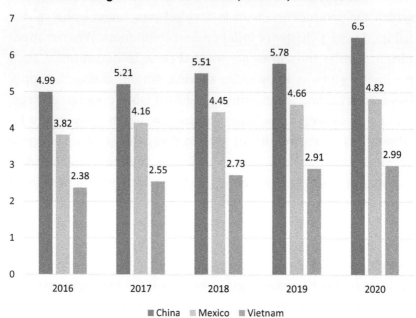

outsourcing to distant, low-cost countries. The increasing number of risks in any multi-tier supply chain – including weather, cyberattacks, natural disasters, and government instability – is casting a shadow on the benefits of low-cost labor, particularly in industries such as apparel, toys, and consumer goods.[13]

China is already being displaced as a source of low-cost labor in some industries, although it remains the core location for much high-volume manufacturing. As shown in figure 3.1, the average wage rate in China in 2020 was $6.50 an hour, compared to $4.82 in Mexico and $2.99 in Vietnam.[14] What then will come of low cost-labor, particularly in categories including retail goods and apparel?

For low-cost countries to be able to continue to grow as export hubs for the world, they will need to improve transparency and visibility of flows. In the short term, the headwinds facing the global fashion industry are having devastating effects on countries such as Bangladesh, for which 85 percent of export earnings are tied to clothes. In Cambodia, one in five households has at least one garment worker, and 75 percent of exports are garments, footwear, and travel bags. Vietnam and India are also top exporters, according to estimates by the World Trade Organization.[15] The flow of apparel from low-cost countries could be significantly reshaped by the pandemic. One possibility is that this may move apparel manufacturing toward a two-tiered supply chain, one that is both "low [cost] and slow" (i.e., produced through low-cost labor and shipped by ocean freight) and a second, mass-customized tier that targets higher-cost mobile technologies with last-mile one-hour delivery, such as the emerging fashion hub located in Detroit, Michigan.[16] Who knows?

The Next Industrial Evolution and Productivity Jump

A second prediction related to supply chain flows is that there will be increased compression of information between nodes in the supply chain through digital transformation and transaction automation. This will lead to the greatest jump in productivity since the twentieth century. The improvement will occur not in the supply chain but between the trucks, warehouses, trains, distribution centers, and last-mile delivery sites around the world.

During COVID, people became more aware of the ability of supply chains to cause things to go wrong. However, many people probably have only a vague notion of what supply chains are and generally associate them with driverless vehicles or tracking shipments on their FedEx app. They often have the impression that e-commerce providers rely on sophisticated customer order fulfillment technology, which is true in many cases. Such myths as driverless vehicles and creating faster port operations overnight were demystified in a recent op-ed in the *Washington Post* by Handfield.[17]

The reality is that if one looks behind the curtain at transportation providers behind the e-commerce order-taking machines, there really is not as much sophisticated technology as you might think (reminiscent of the Wizard of Oz behind the curtain). Most of the activity that occurs behind the scenes in all stages of the supply chain involves human activity, processing transactions on screens and Excel spreadsheets used to make things happen. The next great leap in productivity will be to drive efficiencies in global supply chains, which is the last untapped frontier. There are few efficiencies to wring out of manufacturing plants, but there are massive white space opportunities in the global supply chain. This is also the area where there is the greatest resistance to change. People who work in supply chains do not want to yield control to machines and will block machine-based decisions that take away their spreadsheets.

The next era of change will make supply chains as efficient as manufacturing plants are today. This change will require managers who are bold and willing to take risks, who will hand over autonomy of decisions to machines. For example, when there is an increase in the lead time required to order and ship a part from a supplier, a human planner might decide to increase the minimum order quantity in the planning system manually. But this requires the planner to be made aware of this change, perhaps get approval for the decision, and enter it correctly into the planning system. A machine would do this instantly in response to any changes occurring in the ecosystem. A machine would also be able to link increases in finished goods inventory to planned reductions in incoming raw material inventory for a product line, and optimize working capital holdings.

At Flex, the workforce in managing the supply chain was 8,000 people, with a total supply chain budget of $100 million a year. Tom Linton estimates that 6,000 out of the 8,000 people in the supply chain were in execution, manually reviewing and entering data into computers. Even though many of these were lower-cost workers in places such as India, China, and Mexico, it was still 30 percent of an annual $100 million budget. Reducing the number to 2,000 to 3,000 people would save $20 million a year and improve the velocity of the working capital in the system.

Organizations that employ the natural laws of design dictated by the "invisible hand" of the market, first advocated by Adam Smith, can better predict and develop strategies around the dynamics and evolutionary flow of activity in a particular channel. Moreover, it is important to monitor the total cost of globalized supply chains and model how government mandates, harmonized tariffs, and country-of-origin requirements dictate the emergence of new and unanticipated costs. Executives must be able to weigh production in a low-cost country against the hidden costs of poor quality, late delivery, supply chain disruption, government tariffs/export controls, and the impact of social compliance on the brand. These costs must be modeled using a risk portfolio approach that ultimately considers the total cost of ownership associated with sourcing from one or more countries. Surprisingly, few organizations take the time to work through such scenarios, and decisions are often tactical and short term in their outlook.

Understanding the evolutionary flow of supply chains is made possible through digital technologies that show what is going on in real time. Just as geologists study sedimentary core samples of sand and use this information to predict how a beach will accede or recede, supply chain managers can employ machine-based learning and algorithms to look for visualization patterns. By studying these patterns, they can extract insights into what *is* happening and predict what *will* happen. The next three case studies describe how certain supply chains are likely to evolve.

Case Study 3: More Automation in the Protein Supply Chain

All proteins and meats fall evenly into two primary channels: food service or retail (grocery stores). During the COVID crisis, most food services for large providers, such as school cafeterias, university dormitories, and industrial cafeterias, were shut down due to stay-at-home orders. Some fast-food restaurants still offered drive-through and carry-out service, but the net effect was to diminish overall food-service volume. Meanwhile, more people than ever were buying meat from grocery stores as a general panic emerged in the United States that the supply of meat would run out – a phenomenon known as *perceived scarcity*. As a result, the grocery/food-service market share, which in normal times is about 50/50 in percentage terms, shifted to 70 percent retail and 30 percent food service. The supply chain, however, had been so focused on efficient and low-cost delivery that meat providers could not easily or immediately switch deliveries from food-service outlets to grocery stores. For example, meat for food service is packaged in large quantities, and the cuts of meat are often different.

Further complicating shifts in the meat delivery chain, processing and packing plants such as JBS USA, Smithfield Foods, and Tyson Foods experienced significant shutdowns when workers on these premises contracted the virus. Even plants that remained open had to reduce production to keep workers at safe distances from each other. Meanwhile, exports of meat were also surging.[18]

This situation led Kenneth Smith, president and CEO of Smithfield Foods, to announce: "The closure of this facility, combined with a growing list of other protein plants that have shuttered across our industry, is pushing our country perilously close to the edge in terms of our meat supply. It is impossible to keep our grocery stores stocked if our plants are not running. These facility closures will also have severe, perhaps disastrous, repercussions for many in the supply chain, first and foremost our nation's livestock farmers."[19] This statement further set off media panic along with massive purchases and hoarding of meat by consumers.

Many meat-packing facilities were closed for several weeks during April 2020, reopening slowly despite worker and union concerns. What became apparent was that meat-processing workers were the critical bottleneck in the supply chain. Workers in these facilities often have to stand shoulder to shoulder doing largely manual labor – a job environment that puts them in danger of disease and injury. Meanwhile, there was no shortage of hogs, chicken, or cattle; in fact, many farmers were forced to euthanize large herds of animals that they could no longer sell.[20] No one anticipated that worker illness would affect multiple processing facilities concurrently, shutting down more than 25 percent of capacity for the national protein supply chain. Yet, this scenario could easily have been predicted.

We are already witnessing experimentation with "robot butchers"[21] that can automate meat processing, which will no doubt spur innovation in this space to reduce reliance on human meat processing. This is also an opportunity for other plant-based protein providers, such as Beyond Meat, to step in with meat alternatives.[22] In addition, digital compression will be better able to link growers of beef, chicken, and pork to market demand and allow improved planning and coordination farm to fork.

Today this market is in the throes of a major transformation because COVID exposed the massive weaknesses in the flow of proteins to the market. New forms of protein, such as Real Meat, are also becoming more popular. The flow of supply chain evolutionary design is at work in this industry, which will become more automated and produce alternative forms of protein for a world that is becoming more economically wealthy and able to afford it. Those that survive in this supply chain will need to learn from the hazards of the COVID crisis and adjust the entire food chain to adopt more automated work and flow between growers, producers, and retailers.

Case Study 4: An Evolution in Medical Supply Chains Driven by COVID

When COVID arrived in the United States in February 2020, federal officials largely dismissed it as non-threatening. However, as the virus quickly spread in Washington, New York, San Francisco, and New Orleans, the Trump administration realized that the coronavirus would not magically disappear. As the number of people coming into ICUs escalated, one of the first signs of distress was a lack of ventilators for patients with significant breathing problems.[23] Information we gleaned from several task forces, public forums, and webinars, as well as from personal emails, revealed a pattern of misaligned responses by federal, state, and local governments that created significant health and economic problems in the United States. Observations summarized from these notes are shown in box 3.1.

Box 3.1. Issues Observed during COVID Response, February–May 2020

- A singular lack of federal-level market intelligence left the government ill-prepared to act early with supply chain planning activities for critical materials.
- A lack of technology to enable material visibility led to a lack of insights about where material was most needed. As a result, manufacturers were largely unable to detect in which hospitals there were shortages in critical personal protective equipment (PPE) and other supplies.
- The pandemic supply chain for key materials relied on suppliers that were primarily concentrated in China, which was then curtailing exports of these materials for its own use.
- Lack of coordination among the Federal Emergency Management Agency (FEMA), Department of Homeland Security (DHS), Defense Logistics Agency (DLA), and other federal agencies led to confused communication regarding the distribution of materials, test kits, and therapies.
- A lack of planning and acquisition capability in many government organizations created a poorly executed pandemic supply chain response.
- Reactionary planning and interventionist strategies in the private sector sought to fill the gap for many categories of material that were otherwise unavailable.
- No comprehensive shortage forecasts were developed.
- A lack of visibility into critical inventory at hospitals and long-term care facilities led to disjointed allocation, leaving many smaller hospitals with severe shortages.
- The strategic stockpile was essentially depleted by late February, and acquisition officers were unable to replenish supplies due to the aforementioned factors.

- Multiple shortages of critical hospital supplies escalated the number of deaths, exposed healthcare workers to disease, and further hindered the US medical response.
- Agencies at the federal level competed over decision rights and ownership of issues in a power grab, leaving fewer resources to handle major issues.
- State-level procurement was uncoordinated, which led to hoarding and gaps in material and personnel throughout the country, often with large states getting first priority while smaller states could not acquire supplies.
- National stockpile personnel did not have a clear picture of where supplies were located and could not detect expiration dates on prescription medicines, masks, and equipment.
- The lack of a government barcoding system prevented tracking of material in the transportation and warehouse supply chain. Manual processes were prone to human error.
- Shortages of strategic human capital for analytical assessment, supply chain planning, acquisition, contracting, and logistics were apparent at the state and federal levels.

These outcomes revealed a significant gap in federal and state capabilities to respond to a national pandemic, which continues as of the writing of this book. Poor supply chain design is primarily to blame here: shortages are caused by several inherent problems that exist not just with our national pandemic response function but also with the US healthcare system in general. We observed an ineffective interface between healthcare supply chain managers and clinical managers, which was compounded by a singular lack of a governance structure. This disconnect has evolved to some extent because hospitals have outsourced their procurement of materials to the lowest-cost provider, often relying on third-party distributors and group purchasing organizations to take over these functions.

Information is the most valuable commodity in a national epidemic. Decisions can be made only when information, captured through product barcodes, track-and-trace capabilities, and control towers, is available, allowing companies to see the current state of material in their supply chains. This information is available through inexpensive technology, most of which has been around for 20 years or more, so the investment is minimal. The roadblock to creating this kind of visibility is the current mindset in public and private healthcare, which assumes that someone in the supply chain will make sure hospitals do not run out of materials. This mindset resulted in significant PPE shortages, and caregivers now recognize that "the healthcare system failed us."[24]

The direction of this supply chain evolution is plain. What is needed is a wholesale re-invention of the national pandemic healthcare response system, which currently is dysfunctional but never really worked well before COVID.[25] We cannot assume that the COVID pandemic is a once-in-a-lifetime event. Statements from public and private entities have implied that we will get back to normal relatively soon, returning to the old ways of working. Nothing is further from the truth. The post-COVID world will look very different, and it requires a new pandemic and healthcare emergency response system. Pointing fingers at any particular party is not enough; they are all part of a flawed emergency response system that has plagued government healthcare for decades.

The Biden administration and the Senate are already working to create a more agile federal response framework that will be based not so much on resilience, which often implies rigidity, but on national supply chain immunity.[26] Dr. Handfield has testified in the Senate to garner support for laws that will change the federal response framework.[27] What are the components of a supply chain that is immune to COVID, cyberattacks, or any other major disruption to healthcare, food, and energy? A key effort that will also need to be addressed is the lack of a strong cybersecurity initiative in the supply chain, as illustrated by the shutdown of gas pipelines in 2021. Further initiatives on guarding the supply chain from cyberthreats will be critical.

One of the most important components is the Strategic National Stockpile (SNS), which refers to the stockpile of supplies that the federal government operates to support a country in a time of emergency. We propose that the term "stockpile" is no longer relevant. Instead, we should refer to the SNS as a *Strategic National Sourcing* capability, which is less about amassing inventory and more about establishing an infrastructure for supply chain immunity.

We believe that four key attributes of an immune national emergency response system will evolve: flexibility, traceability, responsiveness, and global independence. These attributes would have created a very different picture than the current COVID experience. We predict that significant changes will occur in the way the federal government manages emergency response supply chains, incorporating a new governance structure for overseeing and directing activity between public and private sectors.

Flexibility

A key component of a future healthcare supply chain response is the ability to predict and plan for the requirements of a portfolio of possible emergencies that can disable the US economy. Such an effort requires monitoring systems that scan different portals to understand future medical risks on the horizon and document the required responses and supplies that will be needed in such cases.

Developing this type of flexibility requires planning, effective category intelligence, and strategic sourcing plans for every possible need that might arise in an emergency. The pandemic planning team in such a system needs to devise war-gaming simulations and capacity requirements that span both domestic and global sources.

FDA requirements should embrace global industry standards to create maximum flexibility for sourcing anywhere in the world. Standardization would increase the likelihood of substitute products; narrow FDA specifications limit alternatives. Instead of stockpiling supplies, contractual mechanisms for suppliers should be established well ahead of any pandemic response so that established supplier market channels are available in an emergency.

Traceability

Establishing contracts with approved suppliers is only part of the solution. Appropriate inventory visibility systems and secure distributed ledger transaction channels are also needed.[28] A missing component of the COVID national response was the ability to track where products were coming from, where they were being sent, and who was receiving them. Hospitals were hoarding supplies, just like people hoarded toilet paper, to ensure they had enough PPE, while other hospitals in the country faced massive shortages and had to re-use masks and gowns. Such problems can be prevented with inventory visibility systems, given a trusted network of distributors and manufacturers that employ barcode and QR code tracking of material through the supply chain.

Consumption of supplies should also be tracked at state, county, and hospital levels so that supply allocation decisions can be made in real time based on daily or even hourly updates. This technology is not overly expensive but requires a central governance system made up of critical agencies working together to address information required for decision-making. This should be supported by an information infrastructure that pulls required data into a data lake serving as the single, reliable source. A centralized data lake documenting material consumption rates and inventory levels that can be carefully curated by a centralized group of IT professionals would evolve, ensuring that improved visibility to events would become available.

Responsiveness

A national response system must efficiently make decisions based on data provided by the visibility system. A leadership team cannot manage what it cannot see; it needs clear channels of communication to review data by experts who are best positioned to understand and derive meaning from it. Data on inventory levels, material capacity, materials in transit, consumption levels at hospitals, and unexpected disruptions need to be available in real time, consumed by a team of decision-makers using a sensible governance structure (described later in the book), and deployed rapidly by senior leadership.

Global Independence

Global independence is a key attribute for creating supply chain immunity. An effective healthcare system response requires a number of components that cannot be sourced entirely domestically. The goal should be to maintain domestic sources where doing so makes sense in terms of national security and to create a global network of trusted suppliers willing to become part of the block-chain/visibility network. This may also involve partnering with organizations, such as Resilinc or Everstream, that monitor global events in supply markets and map them to key global suppliers. This kind of mapping can facilitate an understanding of the full risk picture, securing national needs first, with a cold eye on global impacts. However, it also requires having people who know what to do with the early warning signals, how to act on them, and how to put into motion a playbook for responding to these triggers.

Early warning is the key to early action. It can prevent short-ages and capacity problems. The idea is to keep global suppliers in the field; removing them is not only impossible for certain categories of material but may be detrimental to overall supply chain risk. At the same time, we need to ensure that *we* cannot be removed. This policy is not to be confused with base nationalism, an exclusion-oriented, isolationist policy intent on keeping others out. Rather, the goal is to create a network of suppliers that can flex and collaborate through a trusted, co-determined future relationship with a major government agency. Many global suppliers would jump at the chance to join such a network.

Developing an effective pandemic response requires supply chain leaders and government policy-makers to understand how the government and society see a contingency or crisis. Supply chain leadership encapsulates specific recommendations in terms of federal agency governance, technology investments, and changes in the SNS and domestic supply base for critical materials. The public and private sectors should coordinate plans for managing the domestic, pan-American, and global supply chain site picture as well as contract strategies. This will enable us to respond to contingencies in a cyclical, rather than linear, fashion.

Case Study 5: The Impact of COVID on Contracts and Relationships

In the context of the post-COVID era, organizations must rethink their contracts with struggling suppliers. Trade wars and tariffs were the early symptoms of a disease that has had an impact on global supply chains. In this case, the disease takes the form of managers who are not scrutinizing their supply chains with an eye to continuity, sustainability, and risk. It is not surprising that these companies have failed: they were so fragile that a global episode shattered them.

Given the degree to which supply chains have been in the news, now is an opportune time to rethink how we manage our supply chains. In this epidemic, all contracts are obsolete, and the risk of force majeure – an event that is outside a contractor's reasonable control and prevents that party from performing its contractual obligations – is very high. Supply chain managers have an opportunity to expand their role in crisis management, play a greater role at the war-room table, and pay close attention to what is happening in the market. Although inflation is rising, we predict that this may be a temporary issue as kinks in the supply chain work themselves out in 2022 and beyond. However, now is also the time to have conversations with suppliers to find out what we can do to support them because many have less than two months of cash on which to survive.

Discussions with a Bangladeshi factory executive illustrate a typical behavior that left many apparel producers abandoned. Small factories such as those in the apparel industry are particularly at risk. The factory owner has had trusted business relationships with several global brand customers for more than 20 years. He received orders in early February 2020 and, as usual, purchased cotton fabric and other materials to fulfill the orders. One set of orders from a major New York brand was due on February 17, and was shipped to and received by the buyer. The 200-page contract signed by the supplier stated that payment would be made for goods upon receipt. This did not happen.

On February 20, the buyer emailed the supplier and told him that payment would be pending. The supplier got the same story on February 25. On March 1, he received notice that the payment would not be made for another 60 days. In short, the payment term was shifted with no prior notice. This directly conflicted with both the terms of the contract and the purchase order.

The factory owner was shocked. "How could the buyer change the payment terms after I shipped the product, and suddenly cancel all other orders that were already in production in my factory, for which I have already bought and paid for materials?" he asked. "This buyer didn't even call me to discuss the issue. He could have called me, and we could have worked something out, and found a way to delay payments, hold the inventory in stock for a period, take a partial shipment, or other arrangement. Instead, he canceled more than $4 million of orders and informed me in an impersonal email. This is a lesson I will never forget, as you disrespected me, and our trust is broken."

This story has been repeated by brands all over the United States and Europe, which have completely ignored the plight of their suppliers. Although retail brands are still struggling – for example, the bankruptcy of JCPenney – some action must be taken to prevent a humanitarian disaster.

When demand drops precipitously, and the economy remains on life support for an extended period, it is time to invest in securing supply. This means paying suppliers on time, in cash, supporting critical suppliers' working capital, and renegotiating bad contracts across the board. Banks will need to establish trade financing to support suppliers with working capital support.

Supply chain executives must work closely with their legal counsel and CFOs to re-set supplier relationships and develop new working models based on mutual needs. In addition, they need to set realistic expectations, look at ways to lower cost, and provide encouragement to support the relationship. When things change suddenly and you leave suppliers adrift, they will likely leave. Worse, suppliers might no longer be in business when the economy returns. Ironically, the world is experiencing shortages of apparel and footwear in 2022, perhaps because many of the former suppliers did not survive COVID due to brands' pernicious behavior during the crisis.

Contracting for Evolutionary Supply Chain Design

If supply chain management executives are truly committed to moving toward evolutionary design, one of the first major shifts will be in the way that organizations in supply chains define their relationships, as stated in their contracts. The laws of physics dictate that any flow system is destined to remain imperfect and thus will constantly morph to flow better and more easily as a whole. As such, predicting how things will work out over the course of a contract is exceedingly difficult, so establishing agile contracts that can flex under different conditions will become more important in the future.

Flow systems look and function like animals, and the design and movement of animals has always been a puzzle. We noted in our previous book, *The LIVING Supply Chain*, that animals have incredible homing instincts, knowing somehow to travel thousands of miles to return to a single spot on the planet. Salmon spawning in British Columbia rivers, elephant seals returning to a beach in Alaska, and herons returning to the same Midwestern pond they nested in the previous year all have the homing instinct. Animals are living systems, flow systems in motion, with the freedom to change and the ability to adapt their body design over the centuries.

We can also see how physical laws can be used to understand the nature of physical flows. But how do these laws relate to contracts and organizational relationships? In this context, we point to the first law of thermodynamics, often called the *law of conservation of energy*: energy can be transformed from one form to another, but can be neither created nor destroyed. This powerful law states, in effect, that no matter what happens in the universe, the amount of energy remains constant. Energy can change forms and can flow from one place to another, but the total energy contained in an isolated system does not change.

Think of what this means in terms of the entire amount of energy, movement, and effort in a supply chain. Most relationships are characterized by an enormous amount of energy and activity that does not produce any value. In many cases, this is due to contractual language that drives wasted activity. The law of conservation of energy suggests that when force is applied between two parties, that force can either transfer energy or waste energy. In the business world, wasted energy takes the form of lengthy contract negotiations, hardball price negotiations, litigation, and substandard performance. Productive relationships, on the other hand, can result in outcomes that benefit all parties. In this case, energy is transferred harmoniously and diverted to other projects. Many challenges in supply chain relationships exist because of Western companies' over-reliance on rigid contracts, which seek to impose strict conditions on an evolutionary flow of events during the course of a life cycle that cannot possibly be predicted.

This preservation of energy suggests a new type of supply chain relationship. Collaboration is perhaps an obvious and overused term, yet we find that few organizations take it to heart. What if the energy that was consumed in battling other parties in complex contract negotiations could instead be turned to improving efficiency of flow between parties in the supply chain? Customer satisfaction is affected by three factors: the speed of the process, a manufacturer's ability to improve throughput of the right materials at the right specification, and the accountability for how products are produced. The latter is intricately linked to sustainability. Sustainability has to do with the origin of the raw materials, the fashion in which they are fabricated, and the compliance to human rights laws of the fabricator. Problems occur when a supplier does not produce what a customer expected under the terms of the contract. This is often considered a source of contract risk.

Companies spend inordinate amounts of time negotiating what they believe are bullet-proof contracts, engaging legal counsel in discussions of wording and phrases that alleviate concerns over issues including indemnification and limits of liability. These discussions are almost always for naught because they overlook the major sources of risk, which often cannot be predicted because of the evolutionary flow of operating events that occur over time in a functioning supply chain. The major risk in contracts is that one or the other party does not do what it promised – or does not do it in an acceptable way – and it does something that is not directly related to the contract but damaging to the counterparty. Let us talk more generally about what those risks entail.

In the context of a contractual relationship, we only have to explore the background to those risks and consider how to deal with them. If one party does not do what it promised, is it because that party cannot do it or does not want to do it? We also have to think about the environment in which the contract is being written. If you take option A – one or the other party cannot do what it promised – we can ask: What circumstances are preventing that performance? Are they internal or external factors? Will they occur through force majeure? Did the supplier overstate capabilities, or is it experiencing financial difficulties?

Myriad factors may be at work here. If the supplier is not performing to standards, is it because of poor quality? In that case, do we want to use acceptance provisions or payment terms? Is the supplier exposed to reputational risk by employing slave labor or using conflict minerals? Within organizations, buyers and sellers must compartmentalize regulatory, cybersecurity, and other risks; spell out exactly what their concerns are in each category; and identify approaches for risk reduction.

In other cases, it may be that something is happening that is not related to the agreement but is nevertheless damaging to the parties in the supply chain. As an example, when a major supplier has cybersecurity breaches, that may cause concern for your customers. Performance risks, such as doubts about whether the supplier will meet a deadline, can be managed through frequent, regular meetings and problem-solving sessions.

A final contract risk involves suppliers and parties missing windows of opportunity, such as for innovation. In every case, it is important to identify the source of risk, make sure that both parties are transparent about their concerns about contract requirements, and identify a path forward. These steps, if built into a contract, will almost always alleviate problems that occur over the course of a buyer-seller relationship. In fact, we spend far too much time in contract negotiations on consequences of failure. Instead, we need to spend more time upfront on risks of dispute, not consequences of failure. A primary reason for disputes is that there is not a clear path of escalation when things go wrong. Disputes occur when an issue has been allowed to fester without senior-level intervention. However, if a contract specifies formal escalation procedures, including triggers that will tip off senior executives, many contractual problems can be resolved without resorting to the courts.

One approach might be to introduce a wise intermediary, perhaps a recognized industry expert, who is acceptable to both parties. The expert is briefed during the contract signing, oversees the terms and conditions, and is available for consultation if a budding dispute arises. About 95 percent of the time, both parties will accept the third party's decision, even if they do not like it. Hence, employing facilitators during negotiation can help calm troubled waters during disputes.

The governance structure of a contract between parties should also have explicit criteria and triggers that address force majeure. Interestingly, force majeure was not used extensively as an excuse for non-performance during COVID. Near the beginning, many firms sent out force majeure notices, and in many cases counterparties refused to accept them. This is because force majeure is a legal principle that requires a party to do all it can to mitigate the consequences, which was often not reasonable in the pandemic. Many firms instead claimed "impossibility," a different legal principle, which in the end forced both parties to have a conversation they should have had to begin with. Establishing and sustaining supply chain relationships that continue to flow is a critical management priority not only today, but in the future, as increased uncertainty looms on the horizon.

Time for a New Mindset

Changing a company's mindset is difficult. Leaders often have to make decisions that require investment in infrastructure. This may be a CEO- or board-level decision, which perhaps requires a manufacturing footprint optimization study by a big consulting firm. These types of major decisions are often avoided or delayed by companies that already have too much on their plate.

That is an erroneous response. We believe that decisions such as these should be made quickly, using simple logic, without having to drill down into granular levels of detailed analysis. Too many supply chain executives are content to grind away at lowering shipping costs rather than making decisions, even though such decisions will make a big difference in terms of competitiveness. Instead, they might rely on extensive studies conducted by consultants, who are happy to charge large sums to support obvious changes. Moving material is where the money is, and key supply chain design decisions to create immunity must begin to look at movement as the core component of redesign. Keeping material in motion and shortening the distance material travels are the single biggest opportunities in supply chains today.

Moving forward with a new vision to manage supply chains that focus on flow and transparency will take courage and vision. At Flex, when implementing the Pulse, a real-time inventory management system that allows managers to see the entire supply chain in real time, Tom Linton went straight to the CEO of the company with his pitch. He emphasized that the technology was ripe enough to do this, and it was not that complicated. Armed with the right programmers and datasets, application programming interfaces were created to link different parts of Flex's extensive supply chain. The team began to fill in the white space with connected technologies. But selling it to the CEO was critical. As technologies can better sense supply and demand, exploiting this data in a meaningful way will be the key.

When Linton arrived at Flex, his direct reports emphasized that the factories were underperforming and that improvement was necessary. This did not make sense to him; Flex was a pioneer in lean manufacturing and had been improving factory flow for decades. After looking at data that showed the total inventory in the system, he realized that there were only five to eight days of inventory in factories. However, the total days of inventory in the supply chain was 60 days, with 40 days in raw material and only five to seven days in finished goods.

Linton quickly stated the obvious to his team: "You don't have a problem with factories; you have problems with your supply chain." Although hired initially as the chief procurement officer, in three months he was given authority over the entire end-to-end supply chain as well as procurement. All of Flex's problems were outside the factory walls, and by reducing the days of supply from end to end, his team reduced seven days of inventory at $58 million of value per day in two years. The creation of visibility into inventory and material enabled this change.

How supply chains operate digitally will be the next wave of global productivity and evolution, and will create massive change in how machines will interact with one another. 5G and cognitive computing will come together to create an incredible future. It is high time to redesign our supply chains for improved flow, looking forward to the predictable nature of change that will reshape them in a post-COVID world.

CHAPTER FOUR

Compression: The Localization of Supply Chains

We have a supply chain where they're made in all different parts of the world. And one little piece of the world goes bad, and the whole thing is messed up. I said we shouldn't have supply chains. We should have them all in the United States.

President Donald J. Trump, interview on *Fox Business*, May 2020

Donald Trump's odd statement reveals a profound naiveté about how complex global supply chains function; producing everything for US consumers within the United States is completely impossible in the context of global trade. The statement also defies the logic of comparative advantage. David Ricardo, a famous British political economist, first wrote about the concept of comparative advantage in his book *On the Principles of Political Economy and Taxation* in 1817. Comparative advantage is an economy's ability to produce goods and services at a lower opportunity cost than that of trade partners. A comparative advantage gives a company the ability to sell goods and services at a lower price than its competitors and/or realize stronger sales margins.

As an example, France has a comparative advantage when it comes to producing wine and cheese, while Germany is better at producing cars. Both countries benefit from focusing on industries in which they have superior production competence and know-how. Moreover, everyone realizes greater value when France trades wine and cheese for cars, and Germany trades cars for cheese. A fundamental tenet of comparative advantage is that all actors, at all times, can mutually benefit from cooperation and voluntary trade. It is also a foundational principle in the theory of international trade.

This chapter explores the trend of moving from large, heavily centralized production centers to smaller, localized production units, and explores the implications of this trend for supply chain design. The recent shortage of PPE and healthcare supplies across the world raised awareness that the bulk of these critical materials are produced in China, which restricted exports of masks and other goods during the pandemic. The dramatic impact of PPE shortages led governments and consumers to take an anti-globalization stance and start questioning the level of self-reliance and internal security that a globalized strategy provides. But does this mean that we should all move to localized supply chains?

As we discussed in the previous chapter, the trade wars of the last three years, as well as the events that unfolded during COVID, are a function of the natural progression of evolutionary design. Following a remarkable escalation in the globalization of supply chains, this natural flow of movement toward localization is emerging. Is this shift permanent, or could we return to global supply chains again in five years or so? It is hard to say. To a large extent, industry effects and gravitational pulls will determine how these flows will occur. A key force in shaping them is the idea of compression, drawn from physics. We use it here to explain how supply chain flows are changing, especially how they may be moving toward nearshore and on-shore production.

The natural flow toward localization started well before the Trump administration's escalation of tariffs and trade wars. The roots of this nationalistic movement began in 2016, when Western suppliers expressed dissatisfaction as companies out-sourced their jobs to China. The events leading to Brexit were also linked to UK residents' anxiety about immigration levels. Then came COVID. Some may point to the emergence of the pandemic as a freak event. Given that COVID is an evolved form of the flu, however, it could easily recur on a more frequent (even predictable and seasonal) basis.[1] Perhaps these events are not freakish at all but part of the natural design of global commerce – a frightful thought.

Another trend leads us to suspect that recent supply chain shifts are part of a natural progression. Consumers have become much more aware of where their products are manufactured and of human labor conditions in low-cost countries. Increasing calls for greater transparency, facilitated by mobile technology and cloud-based capabilities, have led to the recent passing of laws in several countries. Among them are the Modern Slavery Act of 2015 in the United Kingdom,[2] the Australian Modern Slavery Act of 2018,[3] and the California Supply Chains in Transparency Act.[4] These laws have created social and political pressure on manu-facturers from other states and countries to examine their supply base in more detail.

Global brands can no longer hide their supply chains behind feel-good web sites. These new transparency and visibility laws require them to reveal that cheap apparel and electronics might be produced with forced or extremely low-paid labor, often by migrant and child workers. Such new requirements are slowly beginning to change the way that production occurs in low-cost countries. Some companies may opt to localize their supply chains or move them to areas where labor laws are stricter and can be monitored for compliance to legal working standards more easily.

If trade wars and the global pandemic are a natural flow of events, are they inevitable? The iterative tendencies of supply chains to seek the lowest total cost can be viewed as natural progression, defined as the flow of goods and services following their natural path. As we noted earlier, when water flowing through a river encounters a barrier – a mountain, woods, or a shift in elevation – it is redirected to a new path. Over time, the river may be diverted to a completely different route. We believe this may be what is happening today: the global supply chain, meeting obstacles such as tariffs and export controls, is becoming redesigned and its flow is being redirected. Ultimately, the supply chain adopts an entirely new structure. We believe that, given the original structure of global supply chains, the obstacles described above are indeed leading to the inevitable change in supply chain flows. We base our conclusion on the physical law of compression, identified below.

> Newton's law of universal gravitation states that every particle attracts every other particle in the universe with a force that is directly proportional to the product of their masses and inversely proportional to the square of the distance between their centers.

This law seems to have a parallel in the supply chain world. Supply chains naturally gravitate to the lowest total cost, which includes not just the piece price but also the costs of working capital, inventory, transportation, tariffs, delays, long lead times, and many other negative aspects associated with global sourcing. The balance of this total cost has begun to shift, not just because of China's increases in labor costs but also as shipping containers and shipping costs have escalated to levels never seen before 2021–2. Global shortages are driving up inflation in multiple industrial sectors in 2022, especially for goods coming from China. To this end, the natural tendency of supply chains to flow to the lowest total cost is driving a shift in global trade flows.

The natural pull of lowest total cost, applied to the movement of material in global supply chains, is causing a substantial, inevitable shift to the flows of supply chains. The cost of outsourcing to distant, low-cost countries has been escalating. This is not just because of labor costs but because of the rising costs of transportation, friction, tariffs, duties, and the perception that insufficient inventory is a major risk that will shut down a business. The PPE shortage further escalated this perception. Thus, the movement toward localization is a natural outcome; force and pressure are applied as the economic landscape changes.

To explore this phenomenon, consider the case of mobile phone technology. Local producers in India and China have taken massive market share by moving toward regional supply chains that produce locally for local markets. This is related to the idea that proximity drives lower cost. It explains why phone manufacturers are taking market share in China: they are closer to customers and the point of sale. For the same reason, Amazon is opening distribution centers close to the point of sale, the customer's home, in the United States. In addition, with the exception of Costco, most retailers are moving to a same-day or next-day logistics delivery model.

Physical compression and localization of supply have many common attributes. Because heavy things are more expensive to move, we find that localized production of heavy products, such as vehicles and erected steel fabrications, is much more cost effective. On the other hand, small, high-value items, such as semiconductors and electronics, can be shipped economically through air freight. Therefore, it is more cost effective to produce these items in low-cost countries. Notice in figure 4.1 that higher-value items make up the bulk of air shipments but that items in short supply during the pandemic, including pharmaceuticals, are now much more likely to be shipped by air freight.

We are also seeing increased functionality in products as they get smaller due to innovations in chip technology. Mobile phones are replacing laptops to access the internet, but they are also being used to control the temperature in your home, locate your car, and share videos and photographs. Likewise, increased functionality is being packed into automotive dashboards, fitness equipment, vacuum cleaners, thermostats, and just about everything. Supply chains reap the benefit of that change, but at the same time, they struggle to transport large, high-cost products regionally. For instance, GE is building the largest windmill in the world in the Netherlands, with blades the size of three football fields. Instead of manufacturing the parts in the United States, GE built a factory in France to produce the blades because they are too big to ship cost effectively.

This is an illustration of the physics of supply chains in action. Supply chain costs are determined by parameters such as weight, mass, size, and distance; logistics costs are based on cubic feet and volume. Reducing any one of these parameters reduces cost and waste and increases speed. Reducing the volume of ocean cargo creates less carbon footprint damage in addition to increasing speed. Research shows that ocean shipping is only three percent of the world's carbon footprint today, but could escalate to 17 percent by 2050 due to the huge amount of

FIGURE 4.1. *Likelihood of using air freight to ship: Year-over-year change*[5]

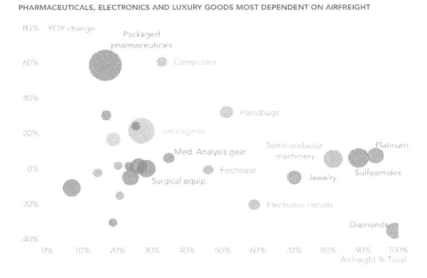

PHARMACEUTICALS, ELECTRONICS AND LUXURY GOODS MOST DEPENDENT ON AIRFREIGHT

Chart compares U.S. imports from the EU based on change in 2019 and airfreight as a proportion of total imports. Bubble size denotes value of imports, color denotes industry.
Source: Panjiva

fuel it consumes.[6] The number of ships waiting to be unloaded outside the Los Angeles harbor in December 2021 created more than 100 tons of pollutants per day.[7]

Organizations that understand the natural laws of design will allow the invisible hand of the market to help them understand the dynamics and evolutionary flow of a particular channel. This information, along with total cost analysis, will help managers decide which types of products and services need to be localized. Forward-thinking executives realize that costs are low in some countries for reasons such as poor quality and late delivery, which in turn can have an impact on the brand and produce supply chain disruptions. These undesirable effects are ultimately reflected in the total cost equation, assuming one is using the right parameters. In addition, as unsafe and inhumane working conditions are becoming more regulated by governments around the world, and being broadcast to the world, the cost of inhumane supply chains will become much more apparent.

As these product and supply chain design shifts occur over time, the evolutionary flow of supply chains will be altered and will continue to evolve. It is important to realize that the fall-out from the trade wars and COVID is re-shaping how global companies do business for the long term. The move toward localization of global supply bases has already begun in reaction to the events of 2016–21. Further, the laws of compression and flow play a key role in several major changes underway in the manufacturing and supply chain world. These include (1) re-emerging lean supply chains, (2) localized healthcare systems, (3) localized warehouse and distribution centers, and (4) automated supply chains.

Bullwhips Escalate When Supply Chain Compression Is Low

Supply chains that evolve are naturally a function of executives who innovate. As discussed in chapter 3, an example is the movement of garment production from China to Bangladesh. Although many apparel manufacturers had already pulled out of China before the coronavirus hit, they still relied on that country for intermediate goods, which threatened to shut down their supply chains when the virus struck.[8] It is likely that intermediate goods will move out of China as well over time, as coronavirus-induced supply chain shortages spread. Such are the natural flows that accompany change, and creative forces are triggered by such discontinuities in supply.

Because global change is inevitable, Dr. Bejan[9] points out that evolutionary design is required to adapt to the shifts that occur in supply chain ecosystems.

Evolutionary design requires individuals to constantly look for emerging patterns in how material moves through their supply chains. Force or action must be taken to change the path of supply chain flows, compress the amount of time that inventory remains in the system, or affect how cash is consumed over time. Pioneers of lean supply chains sought to develop nearby suppliers, especially in the automotive and electronics sectors. Over time, however, the appeal of low-cost production in Asia lured many Western manufacturers to seek production overseas. These extended supply chains are the equivalent of systems with low compression. In other words, they are extended, with long lead times, opaque visibility and tracking systems, and lots of inventory spread out through the transportation and logistics system. The links between nodes are often tenuous and not well understood.

The significant cost advantage of manufacturing in Southeast Asia has appealed to procurement executives over the last 40 years. Original equipment manufacturers (OEMs) and their tier-1 suppliers became overly dependent on extended global supply networks. But recent geopolitical events have started to change the playing field. For instance, increasing transportation costs, environmental considerations, and the resurgence of trade tariffs as nations try to improve their economic position have accelerated reshoring, in which large Southeast Asian OEMs are establishing themselves in countries such as Mexico. This move positions them to maximize access to the North and South American domestic markets, while maintaining the product design and supply advantages they developed in their home base. Mexico also offers the benefit of free trade agreements with more than 57 countries, making it a hub for automotive manufacturing.

Some outcomes of having distant suppliers with extended supply chains to Asia (with low compression) were lack of information sharing, long lead times, and what is known as the *bullwhip effect*. This concept, introduced by Forrester (an economist),[10] is foundational to the operations and supply chain management discipline. The bullwhip effect occurs when an unforeseen spike in consumer demand travels upstream through the supply chain, amplifying its effect due to excessive safety stocks built up by cautious material managers. The consequences are negative: short-term product shortages, overproduction in response, and logistics bottlenecks. The coronavirus not only affected supply due to supplier shutdowns but also increased demand for certain products, which most industries did not anticipate in February 2020. Because more people were staying in and working from home or being quarantined, a lot fewer people were out in the world buying stuff.

In effect, we experienced a twin bullwhip effect. Retailers – other than supermarkets, pharmacies, banks, and some other essential businesses – experienced a dramatic downturn in demand. This was brought on by lockdown restrictions on gatherings and sporting events, school and university closures, social distancing, and movement limited to essential journeys only. With consumer demand down, retailers ordered less from wholesalers, wholesalers ordered less from manufacturers, and manufacturers ordered less from suppliers. As a result, many non-food or pharmaceutical manufacturing firms faced a 60-day lag in the supply of materials, as well as a shortage of workers, ancillary staff, and logistics and warehousing capacity. At the same time, their demand was taking a hit from decreased consumer buying, social distancing, and isolation.

On top of that, consumers were behaving irrationally, stockpiling meat, toilet paper, masks, and hand sanitizer, which made demand curves increasingly erratic for these items. Much consumer buying was driven by panic. Perceptions of scarcity, driven by the mainstream and social media, which miscommunicated information, created uncertainty in product demand curves. Another interesting dynamic was that individuals started spending lavishly on renovating their homes as they sought a work and living environment that was pleasant and modern. This resulted in significant construction cost increases, high demand for appliances and lumber, as well as shortages of skilled trades in construction.

Thus, in the first few months of 2020, uncertainty in supply chains created multiple bullwhip effects. The supply chain of the manufacturing sector was faced with collapsing demand for some products as well as demand explosions for food, cleaning products, and pharmaceuticals. In addition, there were massive shortages of parts, tools, workers and ancillary staff, PPE (face shields, gowns, gloves and masks), and other supplies needed to keep hospitals and production facilities clean, safe, and secure. Panic buying was also driven by forecasts for a dramatic shortage of ventilators and hospital beds for the millions of people who entered hospitals and required pulmonary support systems.[11]

As shown in figure 4.2, exports fell off a cliff during the first quarter of 2020 and started up again when suppliers of PPE began shipping in April. These shipments unfortunately included many masks that failed to meet NIOSH N95 standards and in some cases that were produced by counterfeiters and brokers seeking to exploit the situation. Pharmaceutical imports also dropped from major manufacturers in India and Eastern Europe, resulting in significant drug shortages, particularly for injectables and generics, as well as medications used in hospital ICUs. The drop in US imports of foreign products was further exacerbated by ongoing 301 tariffs during this period (see figure 4.3), which further harmed demand due to higher prices created by tariffs passed by the Trump administration in 2019.

FIGURE 4.2. *US imports: January to April 2020*[12]

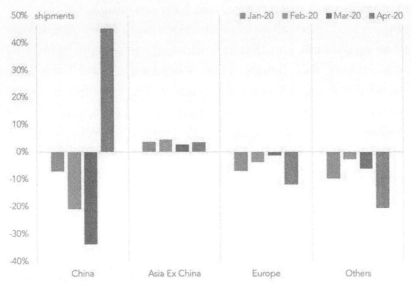

Because 90 percent of the world's supply of PPE is manufactured in China, hoarding occurred in many countries between February and April 2020. Governments struggled to ascertain true demand and supply in a confusing market without a central data collection point. Collaboration between nations ground to a standstill, as leaders frightened by scarcity began stockpiling supplies and forbidding exports of key materials.

Why did this happen? Once again, we return to the observation that purchasing executives are generally rewarded based on one directive: buy it cheaper, from anybody, whenever possible. Low price is often the dominant performance outcome measured for purchasing leaders. In short, part of the supply manager's gestalt is to focus on a negotiated savings of five percent to 10 percent for logistics or purchase price and not to strive for anything

FIGURE 4.3. *Year-over-year change in dutiable vs. non-dutiable US imports: Q1 2018 to Q1 2020*[13]

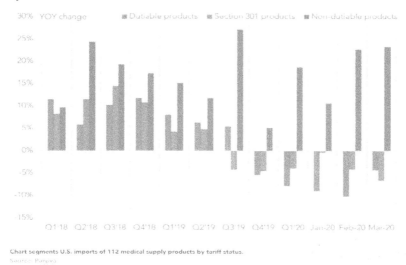

Chart segments U.S. imports of 112 medical supply products by tariff status.
Source: Panjiva

more. The problem is, such savings do not amount to much when an entire month's worth of orders is wiped out by Brexit, trade deal increases, or US-imposed tariffs of 25 percent. When the entire global economy shuts down for two or three months, and people start dying, this economic tradition becomes a lot more than a mistake. It is a catastrophe.

Meanwhile, organizations with more tightly compressed supply chains and who dealt with local suppliers enjoyed a significant benefit during the COVID crisis and were not held hostage to governments of another country. Executives with this kind of supply chain told us that the virus affected demand somewhat, but their supply lines remained intact. During a crisis such as the pandemic, countries became very selfish, as illustrated by the hoarding of N95 masks and restrictions of exports by more than

27 countries. When it comes to a pandemic, governments become surprisingly unwilling to collaborate and help each other out.

The pandemic created a unique outcome: a downstream-demand-driven variation, an upstream supply shortage bullwhip effect, and renewed managerial interest in supply chain designs that integrate lean, local production systems. As one major manufacturer noted:[14]

> Approaches to mitigate bullwhip effect vary, but the fundamental problem to solve is to shorten overall end-to-end lead time from order to shipment. This will require a resurgence in manufacturing and a rebuilding of manufacturing operations know-how on a competitive level that can out-strip any re-shored Southeast Asian supplier. We have to think in terms of "lean" and adopt process automation (physical and transactional). It is possible to change the game; most Chinese factories are highly productive and quality is excellent. However, they still rely on highly skilled engineers performing planning and automatable tasks; this is a legacy we can leap-frog. We will have to have industry-sector initiatives, including partnerships with local government and education establishments to pull it off. The post-pandemic might be the opportunity we need for a lean manufacturing renaissance, re-applying the principles we adopted in the 1980s, but in a new and innovative way.

Lean Supply Chains Increase Compression[15]

A common perception in the public media was that just-in-time supply chains were the root cause of massive shortages of healthcare supplies and missed deliveries.[16] This is not at all the case, and it fails to consider the broader and more holistic meaning of lean supply chains. The principles of lean advocate free flow of information, agile and quick response, visibility into demand, pull systems, and real-time response to shifts in demand. These are precisely the factors that needed to be in place[17] in the pandemic response but were lacking. Yet, many of these principles were shunned in favor of extended global supply chains in pursuit of low landed-cost items. One executive we interviewed noted:[18]

> It's as if we have forgotten about the principles of lean manufacturing and the theory of constraints. We've stripped our own industry of lean expertise, and put the accountants in charge. If the only differentiating factor is labor, and manual labor is taking on ever-decreasing importance, local (or domestic) supply and manufacturing should win. Furthermore, local manufacturing will be less subject to the vulnerability of the extended lead time associated with a global supply network.

Admittedly, we are now seeing a limited resurgence of lean, efficient manufacturers, but in most cases this has been very little and too late. The lean principles of material velocity and shared information in extended global supply chains were noticeably absent during the Western COVID response, and there was very little visibility into the current status of where our shipments were in transit. Everyone during this period felt that someone, somehow, would take care of healthcare supplies. During Rob Handfield's testimony to the Senate Committee on Homeland Security on May 19, 2021, he noted that "America's exceptionalism became America's hubris." The smug, confident ability in US global supply chains turned to incredulous disbelief as waves of shortages of medical supplies spread out around the country.

In addition to initial disruptions from parts suppliers in China, supply chains with manufacturing hubs in Europe, Asia, South

America, and Mexico faced industry-wide shutdowns due to sickness. This situation was exacerbated by embargos on air travel and port entry. A vice president of operations interviewed during this period noted how a just-in-time supply system worked well so long as schedules remained stable, and suppliers could maintain a healthy inventory of parts at their nearby facilities:

> A major problem is that we are operating with no extra capacity in the supply chain. We have very limited storage capacity near the plant, and neither do our suppliers. Literally, I would ring for a part, and it would be delivered within minutes. We don't store parts in the plant; the only storage of note is with the parts suppliers, who typically buy product in bulk from China and keep massive amounts of anticipatory stock at their nearby facilities. Just-in-time refers to the delivery mechanism, not the inventory stockpile at supplier's facilities.

As we noted earlier, supply chain managers tend to be iterative and focused on making small, subtle changes to their current systems and way of thinking. Often, their primary goal is to reduce the price paid year over year through hardball negotiations with suppliers. This is the antithesis of lean, which prioritizes not the lowest price, but flow, velocity, and freedom of movement. These attributes are closely aligned with the principles of flow and evolutionary design, which espouse freedom of flow as the ultimate force in nature. In the current environment, seeking lower prices from suppliers through strong-arm tactics has proven of little consequence compared to the massive forces of economic disruption over the last three years. In the face of significant global shifts to the ecosystem, iteration on price negotiation is a death sentence. It is the equivalent of doing the same thing over and over and hoping for a better outcome.

Healthcare Supply Chains

One question that came up repeatedly during the COVID crisis was, "Why is the healthcare system so unprepared?" During the SARS pandemic of 2010, executives in healthcare delivery and supply industries swore up and down that they would know better next time. Likewise, government bureaucrats assured everyone that a strategic stockpile would be maintained for the foreseeable future. Then nine years went by, and people somehow lost track of the impact of a major health epidemic sweeping the world. The problem today – having just experienced one of the world's worst pandemics – is that organizations forgot about not only how to replenish stockpiles of critical goods but also how to establish a playbook for handling unexpected emergencies. We all thought the good times would go on forever, and a pandemic was not something that was ever on the horizon.

This is a function of a couple of factors. Stockpiling supplies and/or creating redundant sources of supply is an oft-cited strategy for pre-emergency planning. But the cost of stockpiling is not insignificant; it requires investment in products that go into inventory, perhaps for a long time. Typical inventory holding costs are in the range of 18 percent to 25 percent of the value of a good on an annual basis. This includes the costs of capital, storage, interest, insurance, shrinkage, and obsolescence. In addition, executives are not rewarded for holding inventory. In fact, inventory shows up as a penalty in the form of lower working capital. So guess what? Nobody stockpiled.

The inadequacies of the strategic national stockpile noted in the previous chapter reflect the current healthcare system's singular inability to respond to any type of national emergency. We believe this is due to inherent problems not just with the national pandemic response function, but with the entire healthcare system. We observed an ineffective interface between those who manage the healthcare supply chain and those who manage clinical issues, along with a singular lack of overall governance. Theoretically, the Defense Logistics Agency is supposed to manage the interface between the government and hospitals, but we did not observe this happening. The healthcare mindset, not the technology, needs to change, and this can occur only through leadership that seeks to drive change.

Healthcare is one of those areas in which supply chain stockpiling of goods is absolutely essential to handle the first wave of patients swarming emergency rooms. But it is not a long-term solution – it is like a band-aid that helps hospitals get through the initial wave. What is needed is a more sustainable solution – one that involves an actual playbook for how to handle major pandemics and other emergencies. Unfortunately, the press has devoted significant attention to the lack of stockpiles. Stockpiling is just one facet of broader requirements associated with business continuity planning, including asking such questions as:

- What types of supplies are required?
- What types of redundancies can be identified (e.g., second source of supply, multiple transportation routes, etc.)?
- Who are the critical individuals requiring access to stockpiles?
- What is the right quantity and relative cost of supply and redundancy?
- How will we allocated limited supplies across a network of hospitals, and what will be the rationale for doing so?
- What is the governance mechanism for managing the response to a pandemic?
- What are the analytic control towers we need to monitor critical indicators of what is going on in real time? What kind of risk scenario table-top exercises can we review to understand what our options are going forward?

In 2020, nobody had answers to these questions, and there was no centralized task force planning and creating insights into how to deploy assets. Worse yet, there were few sources of supply market intelligence to identify where production of these goods would come from. Demand models are a good start, but without supply, such models will only predict shortages without offering solutions.

Business continuity planning in anticipation of an actual pandemic is an important strategy made even more critical by the length of time required to develop and distribute vaccines. Isolating a strain and developing a vaccine often takes six months or longer. In the case of COVID, once a vaccine was identified and isolated, some of the vaccine treatments required two shots spaced weeks apart, further lengthening the response time. Therefore, hospitals and organizations should rely on other forms of prevention in the short term.

More mature organizations have developed sophisticated approaches to measuring and deploying business continuity plans. As noted earlier, the costs of doing so are not insignificant. A model to identify the costs of stockpiling and redundant sources of supply relative to the lost wages and productivity associated with employee illness can provide important return on investment projections. The results may convince senior executives that the costs of not being prepared far outweigh the inventory costs of doing so.

This brings up another consideration lost on many executives since the last pandemic: how organizations value inventory, and where that inventory is located. Many US healthcare companies had moved their production to China. However, when the coronavirus hit, China began hoarding products to support its own possible second wave of coronavirus victims, leaving US hospitals short of these products. It is one thing to produce masks, but you still need raw materials. Ultimately, the healthcare product shortage occurred because everyone wanted the cheapest product possible.

The post-COVID national healthcare policy will likely continue to change after the dust has settled. Hundreds of thousands of people will have died; even for those who make it through, lung tissue scarring may hamper their lives. To make things worse, COVID variations are probable.

A recent study[19] found that "pandemic risk may be seasonal and predictable, with the accuracy of pre-pandemic and real-time risk assessments hinging on reliable seasonal influenza surveillance and precise estimates of the breadth and duration of heterosubtypic immunity." In other words, the virus could come back in a different form, but everyone will be on the lookout for it. One hopes that the government will have created governance task forces and playbooks to support hospitals and healthcare workers putting their lives on the line. The COVID experience of 2020 may also result in increased levels of domestic production and a local supply base of critical products, such as ventilators and PPE.

Compression Physics Is Driving Massive Economic Investments in Local Warehouses and Distribution Centers

We are already seeing the effect of supply chain compression in the market for commercial warehouse space in the United States and Europe today. A Bloomberg article[20] suggests that warehouses are now becoming one of the hottest investments in the market. The Blackstone Group LP, for example, is betting $18.7 billion on the shift toward e-commerce.[21] This is a perfect illustration of how the physics of supply chains are fundamental to understanding and enabling the digital transformation that is discussed so often in the press.

The rise of Amazon and other e-commerce companies has increased the need for warehouse space by retailers seeking to expand their digital operations and cut delivery times. This shift toward online shopping is reconfiguring supply chains and shaping the fortunes of industrial landlords, with demand especially high in and around large cities, where e-commerce has taken off fastest. US retail e-commerce sales for the first quarter of 2020 totaled $137.7 billion, an increase of 3.6 percent from the last three months of 2019 according to US Department of Commerce data released in May 2020.[22] Total retail sales, meanwhile, were virtually unchanged, at $1.34 trillion. COVID further escalated the volume of online sales by 25 percent in the first quarter of 2020. This trend has continued as more people work from home.[23] In a recent webinar we conducted, experts noted that before COVID, e-commerce accounted for 15 percent of global sales, but it has since ramped up to 35 percent – effectively a 10-year ramp-up that took place in only three months. This is because more people started using e-commerce for almost everything during COVID. Once they started using it, they got hooked, so these numbers are unlikely to go down.

The economic cascade, driven by the need for last-mile, same-day delivery, is now well underway. Bloomberg reported that an investment manager paid for 179 million square feet of urban logistics properties – the warehouses Amazon and other retailers use to fulfill orders from online shoppers. Blackstone's deal[24] with Singapore's GLP Pte,[25] the second-largest owner of US logistics real estate, almost doubled Blackstone's US industrial footprint. Logistics has become a major global investment theme for many venture capital firms, which recognize the growing e-commerce demand.

As part of its global opportunistic strategy, Blackstone Real Estate Partners (BREP) acquired 115 million square feet for $13.4 billion in early 2020. Its income-oriented unlisted Blackstone Real Estate Income Trust (BREIT) purchased 64 million square feet for $5.3 billion. The properties acquired by BREP were in high-growth markets such as San Francisco Bay, Los Angeles, Seattle, Miami, New Jersey, and Portland, Oregon, according to a person with knowledge of the deal. Properties purchased by BREIT are in the Dallas-Fort Worth area, Chicago, central Pennsylvania, Atlanta, and south and central Florida. Today, Amazon has more than 970 distribution centers located close to large cities, many of them leased through owners like Blackstone.

These trends show, perhaps obviously, that the physics of supply chain dictate that despite the move to virtual shopping and same-day delivery, physical assets are still needed to enable these capabilities. Most importantly, companies need to position material on the shelf in assortments that are aligned with what customers are demanding. And this shelf space needs to be close enough to customers that they can be picked, packed, and delivered in less than 24 hours. This means that warehouse and distribution centers will need to be more plentiful and closer to customers.[26] In the past, companies typically used a single national distribution center, with a three-day delivery time and a five-day average shipment time. In 2014, many supply chains moved to a two-distribution-center model, one in the West and one in the East, which facilitated a two-day delivery window.

Recently, supply chain networks are moving toward a metro orientation, with consumer proximity in the same city. The purpose is to accommodate delivery in one to four hours, small pickup lot sizes, short-haul and same-day or next-day delivery, combined with new and emerging delivery models. This metro orientation is driving significant change in industry infrastructure, and investors are getting ahead of it. The trend also suggests that it will not be easy to accommodate. More deliveries means more vehicles on the road, delivering to more locations, which will clash with laws governing vehicular travel in major cities, not to mention higher carbon footprints. Not surprisingly, there is also a rush to engage bicycle delivery firms such as Deliveroo and Uber Eats, which may become more likely to deliver Amazon packages than food in the future.

The Role of Automation in Compressing Processes and Supply Chains

Compression in supply chains can occur through either human or machine actions that improve the velocity of inventory movement and decision-making. In today's typical supply chain, people are primarily responsible for exerting actions to compress inventory along its trajectory. They are driven by primary objective functions, including increased customer satisfaction ratings, improved revenue, or free cash flow. In effect, it is the humans in the loop who make supply chains move today.

However, with the growth of artificial intelligence, human interactions will become less important. This is because human beings are inefficient when it comes to performing repetitive actions, whereas machines excel in performing them. Machines can work 24/7. Given specific instructions to perform, they will do so without emotion or second-guessing themselves. The next wave of supply chain improvements will rely on an increasing number of application programming interfaces (APIs) to compress human inefficiencies. This force will work independently to ensure improved velocity. APIs make it easier and faster for developers to build products and services, and integrate them with other solutions. APIs are a big part of both the cloud and the digital transformation stories. They change the way companies can engage with business partners.

Consider the following example. A planning manager has to input information into a material requirements planning (MRP) system using a bill of materials. This provides the computer with information on how many components and parts go into the product, where the components are sourced, and how long it takes to get each one once it is ordered. Once this information is loaded into the system, an order for that product triggers a set of requests for those components and subtracts the components from existing inventory. When a reorder point is triggered, the system issues an inventory replenishment request for all the components in the system.

This technology has been used for many decades, and it runs whenever orders change from four widgets this week to five widgets next week. But in supply chains, things evolve and shift continuously. Perhaps there is a flood in one part of the country, or a component supplier has a machine breakdown that delays the shipment of product from four weeks to six weeks. When this happens, the system must be notified that the lead time for that item has changed; perhaps the minimum order quantity (MOQ) also has to be adjusted.

Machines may be able to do this as machine-based learning methodologies evolve. This capability must be supported by technology to scan physical inventory in the outbound channel, measure what is in the distribution center, assess what is available to purchase, and determine what is coming in from suppliers on inbound shipments. The system could then identify gaps that might show how low inventories in one system may not be consistent with the amount of inventory in another part of the system.

The ability to detect anomalies, opportunities to optimize, and disruptions or issues within partner locations in the supply chain that indicate a potential problem is something that machines will eventually be able to perform autonomously. By comparison, human operators often conduct this process slowly. Perhaps they first send an email requiring a sign-off from a senior supervisor to change the lead time or MOQ. Then they must wait for that individual to respond, call a meeting to discuss the problem, and two weeks later finally make the change. In the interim, material accumulates, and shortfalls become even more imminent.

With machines doing the work, lead time for raw material will no longer have to be monitored by human beings staring at computer screens, who must then vet inventory buffers and ascertain demand surges or reductions. One machine could replace several humans doing this kind of work, monitoring all products and SKUs, making the work much more efficient. And while machines cannot make major decisions, they can quickly summarize information in a way that enables human beings to make a final decision. When companies switch to machines and their lead times drop, they will not need as much buffer inventory in their MOQ. For example, if a company has 10 parts in inventory for a 30-day lead time, and using machines can decrease its lead time to 15 days, its MOQ will drop as a result.

This level of machine oversight will not happen overnight. As APIs become more integrated, machine learning algorithms will be guided by human beings who are essentially teaching them how to do their job. Change will occur piece by piece, much like the automation of vehicles is happening today. Many vehicles now have automatic lane guides, can self-adjust as they approach a vehicle while in cruise control, and can automatically put on the brakes if another vehicle approaches from behind when the vehicle is backing up. Cars are not autonomous yet, but parts of their operation are becoming automated. Supply chains will likewise become autonomous step by step.

Psychologist D.K. Simonton describes human intelligence as "a cluster of cognitive abilities that lead to successful adaptation to a wide range of environments."[27] Similarly, machine intelligence must be developed through continuous exposure to external environments; however, replacing the cognitive recognition capabilities of the human brain will take years.

Compression of Global Supply Chains

An important physics principle related to compression involves the evolution of natural phenomena, a process that Dr. Bejan compares to the development of a river basin. Water pushes everything in its way, and a river cuts and builds in particular places at particular times. Viewing a river's path from an airplane, you can trace its evolutionary design in the topography of the land. Rainfall generates an architecture of channels on its way to the sea, but these channels are also influenced by mountains, which rise due to volcanic action and tectonic shifts and are worn away by erosion.[28]

Much of the direction of a free-flowing river can be predicted by another physical law: the law of gravity. Isaac Newton's law of universal gravitation posits that a force exerted by the Earth causes the Moon to circle the Earth rather than move in a straight line. He realized that this force could be a long-range permutation of the same force with which the Earth pulls all objects on its surface downward, including water flowing on the surface of the earth.[29]

This idea can help us understand the market disruption forces of lowest total cost, an idea we proposed earlier. This law has been observed time and again: a significant disruption takes out a major industry player who never saw it coming. We can observe this phenomenon in the disruptive forces of Amazon, Uber, Apple, and other major innovators. People often believe that innovation and cost represent two extremes. This is not the case. In fact, innovation is a key driver of *lower total cost*, which is not the same as the lowest price. Since price is a function of cost plus profit, haggling over price without considering all elements of cost will yield reductions in only one place: profit. However, when innovative supply chain partners put their heads together, the lowest total cost solution will evolve. In many cases, this collaboration yields a higher profit for the supplier and a lower price for the buyer.

As noted earlier, the invisible hand of the market (embodied here as lowest-cost gravitational flows) can help organizations to predict the dynamics and evolution of a particular market.

A senior executive at a large auto parts distributor addressed this concept in a panel hosted by NC State University on global sourcing in an era of extreme uncertainty and trade barriers:

All countries have some level of risk, and we have never felt that there is a "slam dunk" country where you can always go for the lowest cost. Usually there is a reason why there is open capacity in a country. There are a lot of supply-demand economics that come into play for a low-cost country, and it is important to understand the reasons for those economics. We know that many large companies in China have some government backing, so we also seek to understand where they are investing, so we can stay ahead of where production and capacity may be growing. We will also benefit in country-of-origin diversification along with a manufacturer who is our current partner.

We try to do as much work as we can to predict trade risks, but the best indicator of what is happening in the market is to keep track of investments made by businesses and entrepreneurs in these regions. That is the best gauge of where we should be manufacturing. We may try to hedge, but should be watching where these entrepreneurs are putting their money, which countries they are backing. From my standpoint, that is the best indicator of where our production should go, as their understanding is much more acute than anything we can put together, because they are the ones making that capital investment in the country.

Another excellent example of supply chains evolving to the lowest total cost is what happened with Huawei. Contract manufacturers, including Flex, were once major Huawei customers, and Flex enjoyed sales of more than $1 billion to this customer. Huawei's annual procurement budget is $70 billion, and it is not even the largest smartphone manufacturer in the world (that title goes to Samsung). The company spends more than $15 billion on semiconductors alone, many of which come from US suppliers such as Qualcomm, Intel, and Texas Instruments. Other US suppliers to Huawei include Skyworks Solutions and Qorvo (high-end radio frequency technology); Synopsys and Cadence Design (chip design tools); and Google and Microsoft (software).[30] Second-tier US suppliers include Applied Materials, Corning, 3M, and Dow Chemical.

However, when it became illegal for US companies to supply Huawei with parts, Huawei sought to redesign its supply chain. It authorized its Asian suppliers (Taiwan Semiconductor Manufacturing Company, Media Tek, Murata, FIH Mobile Limited [a subsidiary of Foxconn International], Jiangsu Changjiang Electronics, HiSilicon, and others) to increase production.

By the time the US government reversed the ban in November 2019, it was too late; Huawei had already moved on. In figurative terms, the company had moved its supply flow to a new river channel. Reports in 2019 unveiled that Huawei's latest phone, the Mate 30 (whose curved display and wide-angle cameras compete with Apple Inc.'s iPhone 11), contained no US-made parts.[31] While Huawei has not stopped using US chips entirely, it has reduced its reliance on US suppliers. Since May 2020, none of its phones contain US-made chips. These include its Y9 Prime and Mate smartphones, according to several independent teardown analyses.[32]

Here is the takeaway: as product and supply chain design shift over time, the evolutionary flow of these supply chain designs is altered and continues to change. People do not realize that the fall-out from many trade wars permanently shapes how global companies do business, though many companies are beginning to localize their supply bases for political reasons. Thus, geopolitics exerts real influence on supply chains and is in some part responsible for how they are re-shaped.

Not All Global Supply Chains Will Compress

Many wonder whether the changes brought on by COVID and trade wars will prevent low-cost countries from competing globally. This is highly unlikely. Companies' demand for low-cost products will continue for some time. Low-cost countries may continue to evolve, but with increased levels of transparency and visibility as a covenant requirement for exporting to Western markets. We may see technologies that permit a consumer to view the natural flow of materials, with web-enabled cameras allowing them to see where it was produced and even the individuals who manufactured their goods. These technologies are readily available today and in the future will be demanded by consumers who will want to know where their products originated and the working conditions in which they were produced. This technological change is another force that may move supply chains toward a two-tiered structure: one that is "low (cost) and slow" and another with last-mile, one-hour delivery.

Recent research also suggests that supply chains are not compressing uniformly. An article in *The Economist* (July 2019) notes, "Trade continued to grow in absolute terms from 2007 to 2017, but during that period exports in those same value chains declined from 28.1 percent to 22.5 percent of gross output. The biggest declines in trade intensity were observed in the most heavily traded and complex global value chains, such as those for clothing, cars, and electronics. As MGI's Susan Lund explains, 'More production is happening in proximity to major consumer markets.'"[33]

There is clearly some variation by industry (shown in figure 4.4). The clothing sector often moves around, and the car industry is coalescing around regional hubs. Electronics remains in China, although the attacks on Huawei are making this more complicated.

Significant differences also exist by industry. In electronics, for instance, China has a number of advantages, including the ability to respond to online retailers who demand nimble manufacturing. Suresh Dalai, a supply chain expert based in Asia, thinks that demanding local consumers force Chinese clothing factories to remain enterprising and flexible. "In speed, China still has the edge," he said, pointing to its world-beating online retailers, "social-commerce" innovators, and nimble manufacturers. In contrast, factory bosses elsewhere complain of unreliability and low productivity.[34]

"For automotive, we've had a distributed global supply chain for a long time," said Hau Thai-Tang, chief product platform and operations officer at Ford Motor Company. He sees a trend toward greater regionalization, with three hub-and-spoke

FIGURE 4.4. *Market share of Chinese-produced products*

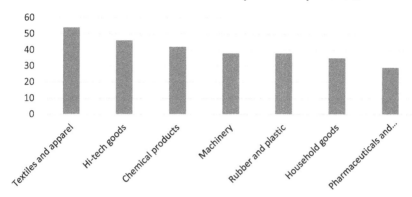

networks: Mexico as the low-cost hub for the United States; Eastern Europe and Morocco for Western Europe; and Southeast Asia and China for Asia.

Car firms have invested heavily to turn Mexico into an export base. The value of Mexico's automobile exports has more than doubled since 2010, approaching $50 billion in 2019. This expansion is spurred by Mexico's four dozen free-trade agreements with other countries, which allow it to export to almost half the world's new-car market, tariff-free. Carmakers have reconfigured their supply lines to take advantage of this opportunity. Mexico's car exports to Germany contain nearly 40 percent German components by value, while those going to the United States contain more than 70 percent US-made components.

Leaving China will not be easy for the electronics industry. Half of the world's electronics manufacturing capacity is based in mainland China. The country's strengths go beyond sheer scale to diversity and sophistication of products. The pace of hardware innovation in China's Pearl River delta is unmatched even in Silicon Valley, as is its unique blend of scale and agility. This is why most of the world's technology giants make their kit in China. Thus, instead of pulling out of China, electronics companies might move to localized platforms spanning several countries in one region.

Years ago, Tom Linton argued that countries such as the United States need to think 50 years into the future, and predicts that the Chinese Belt and Road (CBR) Initiative will become much more expansive. The CBR is a plan to connect Asia with Africa and Europe via land and maritime networks along six corridors to improve regional integration, increase trade, and stimulate economic growth. Africa will likely become the largest French-speaking continent on the planet and will have developed economically and in terms of infrastructure. In fifty years, the United States will likely become a much smaller player in the global economic picture, much as the United Kingdom did in the nineteenth and twentieth centuries.

By looking into the future evolutionary path of global supply chains, it is clear that localization will be key and that market growth will be important in setting the rules. The United States can get bigger quickly by adopting a pan-American destiny, which will involve integrating Canada and Mexico in a more meaningful fashion than in current trade agreements developed in 2019. Mexico has a huge low-cost labor force, while Canada possesses enormous resources, including massive amounts of water and oil, and borders Alaska, Russia, and the Northwest Passage. The latter will likely be ice-free in 50 years, making it a major shipping route. Working together, Canada, the United States, and Mexico could easily leverage their combined resources into a powerful economic force by aligning themselves into a trade bloc. Venture capitalists should forget about investing in China. Today, counterbalancing the size and scale of the organizational design of the rest of the world makes better business sense. Otherwise, the United States risks becoming the next United Kingdom or Portugal, former global powers that have shrunk dramatically in terms of their influence on foreign affairs.

Pharmaceuticals: Lack of Flow Is Causing Drug Shortages

A good example of how misaligned flows in the supply chain cause a ramp-up is the number of drug shortages in retail channels, as discussed in a study examining the relationship between offshoring and product recalls.[35] Unfortunately, the latter are becoming increasingly common and are often the root cause of shortages. A recent study examined more than 1,452 drug recall events compiled from the US Food and Drug Administration (FDA) website from 2012 to 2016. The results suggest that many recalls can be attributed to outsourcing to low-cost countries.

The ongoing problem of drug shortages and drug recalls (still occurring today) is often due to quality problems in outsourced drug supply chains.[36] The underlying causes of these issues are complex. Although there are efforts to serialize drugs (i.e., track them on their journey through the supply chain) under the Drug Supply Chain Security Act, the reality is that we are a long way away from being able to do so.

Drug manufacturing has always been a tricky business. The biggest challenge is that production needs to be controlled tightly through direct managerial oversight. Research suggests that the increased complexity associated with an extended, but financially controlled, supply chain does not lead to lower product recall volumes. Additionally, the study found that foreign ownership of plants may lead to perceptions of control, but in fact the inability to manage communication protocols, as well as cultural and process factors, may exacerbate a recall incident. The results unequivocally show that using a single offshore supplier often leads to difficulties in managing the entire supply chain and reduces the ability to respond to product recalls efficiently. The research team linked product recall difficulties to reduced quality failure detection and consequent product recall magnitude, ultimately resulting in higher levels of products having to be withdrawn from the supply chain.

These observations coincide well with Newton's law of gravity discussed earlier.[37] By outsourcing to low-cost countries, control over a very finicky process is reduced. Think about how little visibility a company has over a process taking place in a different country, with a different culture, in a different language. Both communication and oversight are compromised. Outsourcing certainly works, but the risks of doing so truly depend on the type of process being outsourced and the extent to which it can be easily replicated.

Recent incidents demonstrate how FDA recalls exemplify these problems.[38] Consider the following:

- Since 2018, several batches of three generic drugs used to treat high blood pressure produced in China and India have been recalled because they were tainted with chemicals listed as probable human carcinogens — first N-nitrosodimethylamine (NDMA) and later N-nitrosodiethylamine (NDEA).
- In 2018, the FDA announced a recall of the blood pressure drug valsartan after pills made by Chinese manufacturer Zhejiang Huahai Pharmaceuticals were found to be contaminated by NDMA and NDEA. The drug was sold in the United States by more than a dozen companies, amounting to more than half the valsartan products on the US market.

- In 2018, Indian pharmaceutical manufacturer Aurobindo recalled 22 batches of the blood-pressure drug irbesartan, which also is used to treat kidney disease in diabetes patients with high blood pressure. Aurobindo reported it had found that the drug was contaminated by NDEA.
- Sandoz had to pull back a similar medication, losartan potassium-hydrochlorothiazide, after discovering it was contaminated by NDEA. Losartan, the active ingredient in the pills, was also made by Zhejiang Huahai.

These incidents highlight the importance of putting the right resources in place for supplier quality management. Organizations that think outsourcing is a case of out of sight, out of mind are sadly mistaken. Pharmaceutical manufacturing requires tight control and oversight of trained workers. Outsourcing can lead to communication problems between the consumer-facing company and its manufacturer, and you get what you pay for. Even if problems happen at a very small percentage of plants, once you lose control of a process, all bets are off. You do not have control over what is going on, particularly when you outsource to low-cost countries such as China and India. These factories tend to have high turnover. Sometimes employees are not properly trained, they take shortcuts or do not follow all the steps, and impurities are introduced through chemical reactions and so forth.

In a 2019 report, the FDA warned of significant drug shortages in the United States that would affect approximately 130 drugs commonly used to treat medical conditions or in surgical procedures. The report, *Drug Shortages – Root Causes and Potential Solutions 2019*, provides compelling insights and warnings for supply chain executives.[39] The FDA report states that "56 percent of hospitals reported they had changed patient care or delayed therapy in light of drug shortages." The report adds, "Having high quality quantitative data would help determine which strategies would prove most useful in addressing the problem."

The pharmaceutical supply chain includes multiple players: manufacturers, distributors, pharmacy benefits managers, hospitals, pharmacies, physicians (who provide the prescriptions), and of course consumers. Assuming manufacturers are motivated to produce these pharmaceuticals, what is causing these increasing shortages?

One explanation emerged when we spoke to a panel of executives at a 2019 Resilinc conference. Panelists included a pharmaceutical benefits manager and a manufacturer, who suggested that the drugs most affected by shortages are the generic versions often produced in low-cost countries. Generics sell for pennies a pill, making profit margins very low. As a result, finding reliable suppliers is tough, and in many cases, capacity allocated to these commodity items may be limited, with suppliers not seeing a return on their capital investments. If we want to alleviate drug shortages, maybe we need to be paying more for our generic medicines. At the time of writing, a bill developed by Senator Gary Peters sought to bring back many of the active pharmaceutical ingredients produced in India to the United States to guarantee greater control over generics (which have the most shortages).

Conclusions

One potential outcome of increasing barriers to global supply chains is that executives will rethink their concepts of risk. While multiple risks exist in any multi-tier supply chain, including weather, cyberattacks, natural disasters, and government overthrows, shifts in sourcing locations are likely to increase. China already has been displaced as a source for low-cost labor, although it remains the core location for multiple industries. Our analysis of supply chain impacts shows that COVID-related shortages occurred in electronics, automotive, heavy industry, semiconductors, medical devices, and consumer goods.

We predict the following outcomes:

- Organizations will move toward more localized supply chains.
- Countries will continue to increase trade barriers and tariffs to secure access to local supplies.
- Supply chain executives will focus more on working capital (free cash flow and inventory velocity) as a key performance outcome, rather than on cost of goods sold (low-cost products).
- Automation will speed up transaction flows and increase the need for rapid decision-making.
- Supply chain flows will continue to evolve, using total cost of ownership as the pull of gravitation.
- In general, it will take manufacturers one month to recover from four to six days of disruption.

In the next chapter, we continue to examine the nature of supply chain flows, focusing more on the digital capabilities that lie behind supply chains of the future. We explore the concept of digital dexterity, a capability that will be key to predicting and influencing the flow of evolutionary design.

CHAPTER FIVE

Freedom of Flow: The Adoption of Digital Dexterity

A well-designed flow configuration cannot obliterate imperfection. But it can reduce its global effect so that more useful energy is made available for moving the mass on the landscape. This is achieved by a better and better distribution of imperfections.

Adrian Bejan and Peder Zane, 2012[1]

The discussions that we had with Dr. Adrian Bejan, along with his books, reveal remarkable parallels between the laws of physics and the movement of data in supply chains that we have observed in action. One law of physics involves the movement of matter in a flow system. This movement is measured by the weight moved over distances during the lifetime of the flow system.

> The work required to move any weight on the world map (whether a vehicle, river water, or animal mass) is proportional to the weight of that mass times the distance to which it is moved horizontally on the landscape.[2]

Although the ways vehicles, water, and animals move seem to be unconnected, in fact, all these movements can be described by the laws of evolutionary design as they relate to their flow across the earth. These flows are also predictable and governed by the natural law of speed. For instance, as a river flows freely and forms broader channels over time, these channels are positioned to stay in place for perpetuity, based on a hierarchy of smaller channels that flow in harmony with the large channel.

Dr. Bejan also observed that the degree of wealth in a system can be predicted using the same physical law. A country is wealthy (developed, advanced) because it moves more material and people than underdeveloped countries. In *The Physics of Life*, he noted that the movement of more people to larger cities over time is consistent with the development of societies.

We can apply this physical law to understand and predict data flows in a supply chain. If one agrees that free flow of data is better than restricted movement, it follows that keeping data flowing throughout an organization is integral to improved supply chain immunity and evolution. Dr. Bejan's research focuses on flows in nature, noting that everything flows toward freedom. Rivers flow to the ocean, and all matter flows toward an end state, pulled by either the lowest gravitational pull or by wind and land configuration. This idea of enabling flow is central to this book, as freedom of flow is key to supply chain data dexterity.

In this chapter, we explore the importance of freeing up supply chain data flows and how to do it. We also lay out critical decision-making principles that exploit data through the application of analytics. These skills will be new to many supply chain managers and will require ongoing development and training, even for those of us who have been at it for a while.

As we discussed earlier, the economist Adam Smith in *The Wealth of Nations* (1776) used the metaphor of the invisible hand to represent the unseen forces that control the free flow of market economies. Smith believed that economies should be self-regulating (and thus free-flowing). Left to its own devices, without governmental or other intervention, an economy will self-stabilize: producers will produce according to what consumers will buy, and consumers will consume according to what they want and can afford.

This idea was strongly promoted by some Austrian economists, who believed that the spirit of freedom and entrepreneurship is the foundation of innovation and change. Friedrich von Hayek believed that the prosperity of society is driven by creativity, entrepreneurship, and innovation, and that government restriction interferes with economic freedom and reduces individual freedom.[3] Similarly, Ludwig von Mises, a major critic of socialism, believed that human societies flourish under laissez-faire or hands-off policies, including the unhampered exercise of private property, with minimal government intervention.[4]

Milton Friedman's free-market system principles also emphasized freedom of economic decision-making, noting that a free-flowing economy "gives people what they want instead of what a particular group thinks they ought to want. Underlying most arguments against the free market is a lack of belief in freedom itself."[5]

We believe that supply chains, just like economies, function most efficiently when they are released from constraints and have a natural flow. Creating such a flow requires managers to reduce the constraints that prevent velocity and prevent the natural evolution of pathways that improve efficiency and effectiveness. (Not all constraints can be removed, of course; regulations are needed to guide the flow so they benefit everyone in the commons.) And one of the most important flows that needs to be released is the flow of information – something that many managers are loath to do. But just like allowing funds to flow freely in a free-market system improves economic outcomes, allowing information to flow freely in supply chains creates the most efficient system for operating in a complex environment.

Before the digital age, people relied primarily on telegraphs, telephones, and facsimile machines to share information. Today, the digital revolution allows people to communicate, vote, and make other decisions faster than ever. Although the free flow of information, which allows managers to exploit data for improved decision-making, makes great sense, we find that most supply chains have not taken full advantage of the data available to them. This is unfortunate; insufficient attention to digital information is just bad for business. Supply chains whose responses and decisions are shaped by digital flows are more efficient and free flowing. Efficient supply chains know where to ship products and what styles, SKUs, and options are going to sell better than others. They also can react quickly to disruptions in the supply chain as they occur. Fast-responding supply chains will always beat out slower supply chains.

So why are supply chains in China so efficient? Supply chains operate best in free markets, as we have noted above, and a market economy is like a wild river. When China opened up, the market was chaotic. Eventually, it settled into a calmer, blended market economy, and now it is so highly engineered that it has become machine-like in its efficiency. Its current structure has effectively privileged market flow over human well-being. To return to the river metaphor: the new Chinese economy began as a flash flood but over time settled into a more controlled river, with streams and rivulets that allowed it to flow more smoothly. China's current economy is a highly engineered river, with dams and dykes to improve flow. On the down side, its flow is so unrelenting that it could drown communities or individuals that stand in its way.

Dr. Bejan notes that we are surrounded by patterns, images, and rhythms, which he calls "design." He thinks of design as a noun, a state of being that occurs when something is flowing, and free to morph, like the channel of a river. Design unites the animate with the inanimate, making it an incredibly powerful natural phenomenon. We can see a grand design in the birth and life of a river basin: the rain falls uniformly in a green area, and in time the flow creates a channel in the earth, causing the water to flow in a particular direction and to flow more easily. In fact, this concept explains, and allows you to predict, the construction of all river basins; there is evolutionary and scientific logic to the seemingly random design.[6]

For a flow system to persist, it must evolve so that it provides greater access to its current. Human beings and other animals also are designed for flow. Put another way, animals are made to move. And over time, animals' bodies morph so they may move more quickly, with less effort, across the land or through the water or air. The formula for this speed is proportional to body mass, raised to the power of one-sixth. This formula is universal: it applies to birds, bears, fish, and planes moving across the land, water, and air at any speed.[7] We also may apply the law of evolution and movement to supply chains:

> Flows are predictable. We can predict how they will evolve by monitoring indicators of supply chain activity, using hierarchies of data that have common coding attributes, to understand patterns and enable improved decisions.

If one agrees that evolutionary design of supply chains occurs in response to the natural forces of an ecosystem, then we may be able to predict and envision what the future will look like. Geologists study the composition of the soil and the flow pattern of water in a given area and envision the nature of future flows. Similarly, students of supply chains can envision how industrial flows will be shaped over time. Since supply chain prediction is less scientific than geologic prediction, it may not be as accurate and precise. Still, we can apply the physical laws of flow to project general changes in a supply chain's direction and speed.

It is said that from chaos comes revenue, and from order comes profit. It can also be said that from supply chain integration comes balance sheet optimization. Today, supply chain integration comes not only from physical distance optimization but also from the effective use of supply chain software applications. Freedom of flow in supply chain data is an important metaphor for understanding how information systems can help companies to reduce decision-making time and respond to small changes in the supply chain ecosystem much more quickly.

Digital Dexterity

If free information flow is so important for effective decision-making, then why does it seem so difficult to make it happen in supply chains? What prevents information from getting to the people who make the decisions? And how do we even know whether an organization is effectively utilizing data to predict flows in order to develop a competitive advantage over others in the same market?

The answer lies in the extent of an organization's dexterity and sophistication in employing data and in its cultural embrace of digital capabilities. Data in and of itself is not a definitive advantage. Data is, of course, everywhere; most organizations are overwhelmed by the sheer volume of data, most of it un-used. The key to predicting flows is not data, but knowledge. Specifically, it is the nature of the human-machine interaction that drives changes in a system's design and flows.[8] Informa-tion is not knowledge, and data residing in an organization is not knowledge either. Data must be interpreted in a manner that allows prediction, which leads to individuals who take actions based on data to render it useful. With this in mind, we can begin to understand how the so-called digital transformation of organ-izations occurs not through its data and information technolo-gies, but in the relative level of digital dexterity for individuals in that organization. (At some point in the future, individual in-terpretation of data that requires transactional decisions may be replaced by machine automation, as we discussed earlier.)

Digital dexterity is widely promoted by consultants and think-tanks, but what does it mean? Relatively few managers we have spoken with have been able to effectively define digital dexterity in detail. More importantly, few know how to recognize it in an or-ganization or how to help their employees develop this capability.

Gartner, a business research and analysis firm, coined the term *digital dexterity* in response to the notion that the digital component of most jobs is increasing. Craig Roth, a research vice president at Gartner, defined *digital dexterity* as the ability and ambition to use technology for better business outcomes.[9] Business models increasingly depend on the digital dexterity of the workforce to use technology to drive digital transformation goals.

The key element of any new technology project, product roll-out, or change in the way things are done requires a workforce willing to fully engage with new technology, adapt their work style to include it, and quickly learn how it fits into the overall mission of an organization.

Helen Poitevin, a vice president and analyst at Gartner, noted: "Business and IT leaders need to employ the right talent with a specific set of mindsets, beliefs and behaviors – which we call digital dexterity – to launch, finish and capitalize on digital initiatives."[10] But this still doesn't really tell us how to develop it or if our organization has it!

How Do We Know Whether Our Organization Possesses Digital Dexterity?

Observing how an organization employs digital resources is often impossible for those working within the enterprise. That is because many executives and managers are caught up in the day-to-day activity of their jobs and are often fighting fires without a meaningful application of data. There is no question that most organizations continuously invest in new technologies. But little is known about the ability of the workforce to embrace and absorb these technologies in their daily work. Many workers remain tied up in using email, databases, Excel, and PowerPoint to communicate and make data-based decisions.

In theory, creating digital dexterity would allow every decision-maker in an organization to act on data that provides prediction. This is particularly challenging for goals that cannot be easily measured and assessed (such as whether we've achieved digital dexterity!). Several executives we spoke with highlighted this challenge.

In a sense, creating an analytics culture is about considering opportunities along two dimensions: data quality and speed to value. Where you decide to take action becomes a cultural problem: Where in your company should you begin to capture quality data to drive business results? And how do you get started?

We are in the very early stages of using data for real-time decision-making, largely because many companies struggle with
data quality. It is also very difficult to digitally connect groups
across organizations. Most people extract data, load it into
spreadsheets, and use graphs to visualize it. Digital dexterity
cannot occur until people cease to be so siloed and begin to make
joint decisions using the same sets of data. At one company we
worked with, for example, the security group was not using the
same data as space planning, which was not connected to the
human resource team. This was the case even though an opportunity clearly existed to use data to combine these business functions for aligned decision-making. What is needed is a cultural
shift whereby people in different functions are willing to lose
control of their data by allowing it to be shared with other business functions. Although everyone agrees in principle that data
sharing is a good thing, most organizations display a lot of constraints, often due to old regulations that prohibit data sharing.
In some industries, such as financial services and healthcare, it is
prohibited by regulators. There are some security concerns about
data sharing as well, but cloud providers are developing some
interesting opportunities there. Also, blockchains can be used to
exchange data securely.

At some point in the future, humans won't be making as
many data-driven decisions. Experts predict that 70 percent of
human-driven transactions in procurement will be automated
by bots and other technologies.[11] Companies such as General
Motors and IBM are already adopting these technologies, seeing
them as important components of the future technology environment. However, these technologies will not really catch on
until the biggest changes occur in the mindsets of managers who
interface with these technologies, not the technologies themselves. Until people fully understand how the interface between

humans, data, and decision-making occurs, companies will not have the knowledge they need to establish supply chain flows. Executives will make big technology investments in artificial intelligence, machine learning, and automation only to find that the technology remains idle and unused, with no return on these investments.

Emerging technologies are allowing people to do much more with data than in the past. For example, supply chain risk management firms Resilinc and Everstream provide managers with instantaneous notification of disruptive events all around the world. They map these events to key supply networks, identifying tier-1, -2, and -3 suppliers located in a concentric area near the event that may be affected. While providing notifications of events, the missing link is that managers must decide on their own how to mitigate the impact of sourcing disruptions in different parts of the world.

Armed with this knowledge, managers must then take an action to find alternative supply once they understand the level of risk and disruption involved. In a sense, the mapping of the supply chain is equivalent to mapping the genome; the DNA of a supply chain is being sequenced. Mapping supply chains allows managers to accelerate the flow of material in logistics channels in ways that were not possible before. Mapping and digitizing a supply chain is like moving from an analog to a digital mindset, allowing companies to instantaneously witness events across multiple tiers of the supply base in a predictive and intelligent fashion.

Another metaphor for supply chain mapping is magnetic resonance imaging (MRI), a technology that allows physicians to peer inside layers of the human body and begin to recognize previously undiagnosed conditions and diseases. Similar to an MRI image, intelligent technologies provide analytics that must be interpreted by individuals who have the training and experience to understand what they are seeing. Not everyone will see the information, so they cannot identify whether disruptive issues are occurring or whether the magnitude of potential disruptions or opportunities can be acted upon. But there is an important caveat: individuals must also be able to trust the images they are seeing in real time.

The Challenges of Poor Data in Supply Chains

To be able to rely on digital outputs for decisions, individuals must be confident that their systems are capturing reliable data from the flows that surround them. Two of the biggest weaknesses in today's supply chains are unreliable intelligence and unreliable data. Yet these key indicators are ironically the foundation to effective decision-making.

Allowing one group of people to control data and keep it to themselves can slow down and destabilize performance. On the other hand, if an organization shines a light on data and allows both employees and external partners to view and interpret the information and collaborate in the process, business value is created. While a policy of data democratization makes the organization appear thoughtful and considerate of others in the value chain, it is in fact self-serving: the greater good accumulates to the company that initiates freedom of flow, as it allows suppliers and distributors to produce better and more efficient outcomes. As the entire supply chain becomes more efficient, eventually value is created for all parties but accumulates most to the organization sharing the data. Similar principles are embodied in Adam Smith's invisible hand concept, suggesting that he would have made a good supply chain executive.

An overview of analytics research suggests that analytics and business intelligence have many limitations and challenges to overcome. These are summarized below in no particular order.

Analytics are nascent.

Many functional groups, being asked to do more with less, find themselves unable to keep up with the volume of transactional work. The demand for this work is driven by legacy enterprise resource planning (ERP) systems focused on financial reporting; ERP systems may not offer appropriate business decision support analytics. In most cases, functional analysts are limited to conducting quarterly spreadsheet reports, combined through manual data accumulation across multiple systems. Locating multiple data types in numerous systems forces users to run multiple reports to get an overall view of required information. These reports often require financial and other functional business analysts to manually integrate reports in Excel.

At one American organization we visited, a "Key Business Data" report compilation can often take as many as 11 financial analysts several weeks to complete. According to an MIT *Sloan Management Review* report, "The experience of managers grappling, sometimes unsuccessfully, with ever-increasing amounts of data and sophisticated analytics is often more the rule than the exception."[12] Our own findings confirm this observation.

Data integrity and quality issues are preventing significant advances in analytics.

All advanced analytics require data, and data integrity and quality are essential to their production. Accurate, timely, reliable, and standardized data is essential for taking actions based on information. The adage "garbage in, garbage out" is cited in multiple organizational interviews, yet managers are often unsure what steps are needed to improve data quality. A Deloitte survey found that 49 percent of supply chain officers believed that data quality was the biggest barrier to digital technology.[13] A study by NC State University found that for almost two-thirds of organizations, poor data quality is the primary cause of less-than-optimal supply chain decisions, and that only 20 percent of organizations are addressing the issue through an improvement program.[14]

Internal structured data is often rife with coding errors. Analysts struggle to link data that provides integrated insights into how suppliers, customers, contracts, price agreements, market demand, SKU numbers, market penetration, customer satisfaction, and other factors affect one another. While a magnitude of error exists in any dataset, significant gaps in enrichment of data, as well as poorly defined coding systems, can lead to erroneous summary statistics. These errors can lead to misleading interpretations of spent data.

In one case, a large chemical company has gone through several mergers and, as a result, must manually download data from multiple legacy systems every month. Analysts send the data to a data cleansing business in India and review the financial data two weeks later. There is no unified approach for creating up-to-date performance dashboards or analytics.[15]

Ad hoc approaches to capturing unstructured data must be replaced by a data governance strategy.

Interviews suggest that business analysts rarely have the time to create and enforce a rigorous standardized approach to market research and intelligence. This means that much of the unstructured data available to support market intelligence for buy- and sell-side market development is untapped, unavailable, and in a format that cannot be effectively analyzed. Because companies need the flexibility to acquire this information and structure it for appropriate internal use, data governance is a fundamental requirement.

Organizations need to impose a system of governance to construct and build data for analytics.

It is important to create a structured approach to organizational data that builds on internal sources of business intelligence. The most important sources of data upon which to construct analytics are internal. Among them are ERP data, financial reporting system data, customer contract data, customer satisfaction data, customer relationship management data, project execution data, spend data, and supplier data. Increasingly, however, external sources such as market size/growth, supplier risk, supplier diversity, and external news feeds are also becoming important data inputs to the mix. Historical data sources may include basic product coding, cost models, and contract visibility. These sources must have a strong product and service coding structure, which forms the foundation for other data taxonomies that can be collected in real time and for predictive modeling approaches that will drive an increased level of insight. When integrated in a structured fashion, data begins to become useful as a basis for analytical prediction.

Low usage of advanced analytics is the norm.

As a result of inadequate data governance programs in most organizations, low usage of analytics is the norm. Most organizations struggle even with historical analysis and have few opportunities for broader data analytics across buy-side, sell-side, and internal operation landscapes. Even when there is greater data transparency, organizations are often at a loss as to what to do with the data.

Our experience is that digital dexterity requires high-quality data. Individuals need to be able to trust the data they are relying on to make decisions. If the data cannot be trusted, split-second decision-making cannot occur. People will simply delay decisions until they feel more confident about what the data is telling them.

But what does it mean to have quality data, and what can be done about it? The answer involves establishing a robust data governance initiative to produce intelligence on events in the business in real time. Definitions of data governance, business intelligence, and analytics will be helpful in understanding exactly what is involved.

Data governance: The exercise of authority and control (planning, monitoring, and enforcement) over the management of data assets.[16]

Basic data governance ensures splitting accountability and responsibility for data, thus empowering better decision-making while using data from disparate data sources and methods. In effect, data governance provides a system of decision rights and accountabilities for information-related processes. These processes are executed according to agreed-upon models, which describe who can take what actions with what information, when, under what circumstances, and using what methods.[17]

An overarching governance structure must make individuals in functions responsible for the quality, accuracy, and timeliness of their data because it is to be pooled for business decision-making.

That is, purchasing must be responsible for the quality of its data; finance for its data, etc. Every part of the organization must be brought into the governance effort. Of course, there will almost always be resistance. A common complaint is that data quality is IT's job. This is incorrect. Because functions are responsible for inputting data at the source, they must be held accountable for inputting the data accurately. There are technologies that can help with this. However, the natural flow of data cannot be restricted: the information flow channels that create the right operational and strategic decision frameworks for digital decision-making must be allowed to develop and form.

> *Business intelligence (BI)*: A technology-driven process for analyzing data and presenting actionable information to help executives, managers, and other corporate end users make informed business decisions.

The term *business intelligence* dates back at least to the 1860s, but consultant Howard Dresner is credited with proposing it in 1989 as an umbrella phrase to describe applying data analysis techniques to support business decision-making processes. What came to be known as *BI tools* evolved from earlier, often mainframe-based analytical systems, such as decision support systems and executive information systems.[18] Typically, business intelligence can be used for ad hoc analysis using visualization tools that allow users to create more meaningful insights through dashboards, control towers, visual graphics, and charts.

The goal of business intelligence systems is to create individual dashboards or control towers that provide instantaneous access to operational criteria that define the state of supply chain operational flows. To develop these dashboards, individual users must visualize the desired outcome and the critical leverage points in value chain processes that determine criticality or shifts in flows. This makes sense: to predict outcomes, metrics that define current flows need to be defined, and the right data must be extracted and consolidated to provide real-time views of these indicators. The key is where in the flow to measure a process, and to understand what data is important. Individuals also need to be both vigilant and aware of what types of shifts in data flows indicate problems or opportunities in the supply chain, and pay attention to the type of data that is representative of what is happening in that area of the flow.

Analytics: The outcome of a series of advanced operations performed on data extracted from business intelligence systems.

Business analytics involves a command of science and mathematics, especially of such techniques as data mining, predictive analytics, text mining, statistical analysis, and big data analytics. Advanced analytics projects are often conducted and managed by separate teams of data scientists, statisticians, predictive modelers, and other skilled analytics professionals, while business intelligence teams oversee the more straightforward querying, data correlation, and data analysis.

The Gartner Magic Quadrant report notes that the business intelligence and analytics platform market is undergoing a fundamental shift. Over the past 10 years, business intelligence platform investments have largely been in IT-led consolidation and standardization projects for large-scale record-reporting systems. These efforts have tended to be highly governed and centralized, whereas IT-authored production reports were pushed out to inform a broad array of consumers and analysts. Now, a wider range of business users are demanding access to interactive styles of analysis and insights from advanced business intelligence visualization tools that do not require them to have IT or data science skills. As business users' demand for pervasive access to data discovery grows, IT wants to deliver without sacrificing governance.[19]

The Gartner report also notes that, as "companies implement a more decentralized and bimodal governed data discovery approach to business intelligence, business users and analysts are also demanding access to self-service capabilities beyond data discovery and interactive visualization of IT-curated data sources. This includes access to sophisticated, yet business-user accessible, data preparation tools. Business users are also looking for easier and faster ways to discover relevant patterns and insights in data."[20]

According to a study by the International Institute of Analytics and the SAS Institute,[21] business intelligence adoption is more prevalent across organizations than advanced analytics. The study notes, "While the path from basic reporting to more advanced analytics work is often considered as a shift from BI to AA (advanced analytics), the reality is that advanced capabilities should augment, not replace, less advanced functionality."[22]

Organizational weaknesses are perceived to be among the strongest deterrents to adopting business intelligence and advanced analytics practices across organizations. Data governance programs are fundamental to both business intelligence and business analytics outcomes, because governance is critical to ensuring acceptable data quality levels.

Ensuring digital dexterity also involves speed-to-value, which refers to the dexterity with which users can employ the data and convert it into decisions. This, in turn, requires (a) users who can derive meaning from data and (b) timely access to data in a form that allows easy manipulation and penetration.

The Hinge Factor in Digital Dexterity

An important question to ask regarding human machine-interaction is "Where does human decision-making enter the loop?" A very interesting book that helped us think through this concept is *How Chance and Stupidity Have Changed History: The Hinge Factor*[23] by Erik Durschmied. The author looks at battles that changed the course of history, including the Crusaders' loss of the cross to Muslim forces at the Battle of Hattin in 1187, the defeat of the French at the Battle of Agincourt in 1415, Napoleon's defeat at Waterloo in 1815, and the Civil War battle of Antietam in 1862. Each of these defeats was caused by a blunder, the caprice of weather, or individual incompetence. These unforeseeable errors resulted in the loss of thousands of lives and changed the course of history. We believe that such a hinge factor also occurs in supply chains, when an individual leader must make a critical, difficult decision in the face of uncertainty and limited intelligence, and with significant resources at play. A blunder made at such times can have enormous detrimental follow-on effects on the organization's future.

What is the hinge factor in supply chains? We have explored organizations that are developing global security operations centers, which show incredible amounts of real-time data. One was at Flex, another at Caterpillar, and yet another at Biogen, in which a control room shows activities occurring around the world. Huge maps in these rooms show events such as flooding in India, riots in Hong Kong, and forest fires in California, as well as other disruptions.

Resilinc and Everstream have both developed risk platforms to help customers stay abreast of global events that might affect their supply chain. Such platforms can also link an event to key suppliers within a range of the geographic location and, through a bill of materials, identify the financial impact of an event. What managers do with this information is not prescribed, but requires that managers who gravitate to such systems know how to respond when alerted to a risk event. This is the real hinge factor in supply chain: When is a risk event a false alarm that should be ignored, and when should action be taken by managers? And if action is to be taken, what action is required? Solving risk issues often involves significant outlays of funds, so avoiding risk is not free.

Consider 9/11, when the chief air controller of the Federal Aviation Administration realized that the United States was under attack. His immediate response was to ground all flights, including those in the air. Rob Handfield was on a flight from Detroit to Moline, Illinois, that day. He ended up being deposited in Kalamazoo, Michigan, and had to drive home to North Carolina in a rental car. In retrospect, grounding planes was an enormously impactful, courageous call, and it turned out to be the right one. But we do not have the benefit of hindsight when we are called on to make quick decisions when confronted with risky events.

The benefit of risk management systems is that they provide managers with an early warning – the key in the battlefield of supply chain management. When you can get information ahead of your competitor, your company can move its assets more efficiently and win the battle. This is a real benefit only if we use the information to make the right call. But too many false alarms can be costly if it requires an all-hands-on-deck approach every time. Hence, prudence must be balanced with careful consideration of the facts, to avoid recklessness, abandon, or ignorance of the facts.

For example, the rain that fell on the ploughed ground at the battle of Agincourt did not halt the attack of the superior French army.[24] Ignoring the fact that the battleground had become a muddy mess, they drove in their cavalry, loaded with heavily armored knights. When the horses fell, mired in mud, English longbowmen massacred the French, whose army had 10 times more men. Similarly, poor communication and a lack of critical supplies (in this case, a fistful of nails that would have rendered the enemy's captured cannons useless) led to Napoleon's defeat at Waterloo in 1815. In the same manner, supply chain leaders when facing a risk event need to carefully plan ahead to establish how they will react to unexpected risks, including hurricanes, terrorist attacks, cyber terrorism, and, yes, slow-moving pandemics.

In the remainder of the chapter, we examine in more depth how the combination of automation, digital technology, and human decision-making can align to improve a variety of decisions within global supply chains. We examine a number of cases which highlight the barriers that can hinder even the most careful evolutionary design, blocking supply chain information flow. Most involve human error: the managerial mindset to avoid being blamed for poor decision-making, a lack of data analysis skills, or, in many cases, a reluctance to adapt to changing conditions. These barriers prevent the ideal future state, characterized by managers who are able to employ data to predict flows of materials, people, demand, risk, or any other attribute important to supply chains. These expert managers will infuse their environment with a data-driven culture in which decisions are made based on universally agreed-upon analytical outputs.

Let us examine these challenges in more detail through two case studies that provide insight into how to create a digital capability: Siemens Building Technologies Digital Strategy and Biogen's Supply Chain Operations Center. The Siemens case is an excellent example of a free-flowing data strategy.

Case Study 6: Siemens Building Technologies Digital Strategy[25]

"People initially have many different interpretations of what is meant by analytics," said Carl Oberland, Siemens CPO. "We spent a good deal of time seeking to establish the mission and vision of our digital transformation." What do we mean by a digital platform? What is digital governance and stewardship?

Oberland shared how Siemens decided to build an analytics capability at the business intelligence layer based on the belief that this was the quickest way for a value proposition to emerge, which would get the executive team to want to continue to invest. Since then, their efforts have accelerated, and they have moved quickly into other areas of the analytics space. He notes that "It's great to have a lot of data, but we also recognized it was more important to have good quality data. Otherwise, you have isolated pockets of data that cannot be leveraged across the organization. In a sense, creating an analytics culture is about considering opportunities along two dimensions: data quality and speed-to-value. Where you decide to take action becomes a cultural problem, involving how to drive a change in culture in how we capture quality data to drive a business result, and where to begin the journey."

Siemens refined this question by seeking to create a higher digital IQ across all business functions. One function, that already used analytics, was at the middle school level, while other functions were at the elementary level; the goal was to get everyone to a high school level.

Oberland said:

Creating a data platform was key for us. We were worried that if we just put a bunch of tools out there, it would be a free-for-all, and there would be 10 people working on different apps to solve a common working capital problem. Instead, we wanted to get control of the analytics development process, and to seek to solve problems as a standard for the whole company, to minimize waste.

Our goal was not to move to "Excel on steroids." Rather, we wanted some level of control. To create a more robust BI capability, we also recognized that we couldn't leave this in the hands of data scientists … [who] had a different perspective on the same subject, and we needed to pull these different views into a centralized viewpoint that reflected all these views. This is the vision we sold to the CFO.

Siemens began this journey by focusing on data governance, beginning with core data on customers and then establishing quality data for systems operating in different areas. This required developing regional governance by area, using Hyperion to create financial reports, as well as using a project management tool used at universities and hospitals. The initial goal was to make sure that the team interconnected data from different places while addressing data quality. Some initial disputes arose regarding whose data went into the data mart first. Finance wanted Hyperion data for financial analytics, whereas operations wanted the project management data, so the team had to go through a reconciliation process.

An important component of the roll-out was the development of institutional analytics, that is, analytics with a standardized look and feel. To enable this, Siemens adopted a single visualization platform as the standard. In many organizations, analysts spend weeks establishing their end-of-quarter charts and graphs. The goal was to enable executives to generate exactly the metrics and charts they wanted, any time, with the click of a mouse. Siemens achieved this goal for business intelligence, creating a platform that allows all senior executives to click the mouse to download a dashboard prior to a meeting at any time, not just at the end of the quarter. One executive told Oberland that this capability, more than any other, allowed him to completely change the way he managed the business. Now, sales executives are grilled on what shows up on the dashboard and can be engaged weekly, instead of just at the end of the quarter.

Another type of analytical capability, which applies to only about five percent of the workforce who will become adept at it, involves discovery analytics. This refers to the ability to drill down into datasets and explore relationships. Conducting data analysis requires users who are technically oriented and understand what types of data are required to address a business problem. Another important foundation for discovery analytics is enabling data configuration and establishing an IT resource to do so. Director-level executives emphasized that they wanted to be able to do their own analyses but could not capture the data to produce the analysis they needed. This required mapping needs to data, followed by technical visualization, end-user inputs, and assigning data stewards to capture the data. Pulling it all together was a challenge. To coordinate the movement and capture of data, the CFO established a digital office for the entire organization, which moved the initial effort out of procurement. The program office at the local level handled regional data governance.

Finally, one of the most important elements for creating an analytics culture is a solid technical visual team. In the movie *Moneyball*, Peter Brand (played by Jonah Hill) was the key individual who pulled together all the data required to assess ball players. Every organization needs a Peter Brand: someone who can cover data flowing in from human resources, legal, operations, and procurement and make it usable and accessible for the common manager.

Oberland noted:

When you first approach departments and ask them what analytics they need ... they don't have a clue. But once they get a fla-
vor for how analytics can support business decisions, they want
more. And then things mushroom, at which point you need to
establish each department's responsibility for data stewardship
that must reside within those departments. Getting each department to understand what it takes will get them involved, and they
then become instrumental in picking out which data they needed
to sustain and steward for their visualization requirements. And
each one also identified who the resident data expert and visualization analyst/expert would be at a local level. The local data
steward is one of the most important roles, because this individual is responsible for understanding what data quality looks like
when it's right, and if it can be shoved into the system.

Some fundamental analytics used at Siemens to create basic
but critical performance insights for senior executives include
the following:

- To facilitate a click-of-the-mouse analytics capability, the company developed an institutional analytics landing page.
- Executives can access a dashboards pathway, which is loaded
  once a month. Executives can easily download the dashboard and quickly email it to the executive team for discussion. Some of the key metrics used by the divisions include:
  o **Project risk analysis**: Almost 20 percent of customer field projects
    are high-risk. The new analytics system not only identifies such
    projects but scores their risk level, highlighting them on a dash-
    board by a red indicator.
  o **Forecasting**: A financial forecast provides executives with a trajec-
    tory on organizational costs versus budgeted costs.

- ○ **Visualization deep dive**: To help promote competitive bidding (versus simply awarding contracts to suppliers), an analytical tool highlights the higher cost of those that are competitively bid versus not. The tool increased competitive bidding of projects from 45 percent of the total volume to 70 percent.
- ○ **Contribution to net income**: This metric shows the cost out.
- ○ **Contribution to growth**: This metric allows the company to forecast margins on a project before the job is booked with the customer.
- ○ **Purchasing volume**: This feature allows executives to click on a division's purchasing spend and see how much volume is going to different types of suppliers (minority, women-owned, small business, p-card spend, etc.)
- ○ **Business reviews**: Financial and business metrics are calculated in real time for all projects in a division, including gross margin, absorption, utilization, and 22 other dashboards. One executive noted, "The most impactful contribution to the business has been the BI platform that we developed this year. This has allowed every executive to monitor the analytics important to her or his own business."
- ○ **Budget dashboard**: This dashboard allows executives to understand the current and forecast status of their internal cost center. The dashboard allows them to determine how to adjust salary and fringe benefits to affect the forecast that rolls out to the general ledger, which is sent to finance every month.
- ○ **Supplier risk**: A group of NC State graduate students developed this metric through the Supply Chain Resource Cooperative. It gauges an executive's potential to influence project risk through alternative supply, setting the risk at high, medium, or low. This platform enables a discussion on supply risk with the business and allows the sourcing manager to look at geographic lanes and map the root cause of disruptive events down to component level. This can lead to actions such as seeking a second source or increasing inventory buffers.

Here were a few lessons that Siemens took away from this foray into deployment of analytics:

- **Start on a small scale**. Efforts should be piloted first in one function to understand how to move data into a data mart.

- **Data stewardship and data governance** are the most difficult aspects to establish in any analytics initiative. Establishing responsibility for data quality is key, and the role of the regional/local data steward is critical.
- Do not underestimate the **skill level change** that is needed for personnel to think analytically. Until they see what it looks like, they will be lost, and they cannot tell what types of visualizations are needed.
- **Consider cool apps.** Be mindful of the program becoming another Excel on steroids. This occurs when multiple people are trying to solve the same business issue in their departmental silos, resulting in significant variation in look and feel. However, if someone comes up with a cool app at the discovery level and the business owner likes it, then escalate it. Put it into the institutional view in a standard format for everyone to use.

Case Study 7: Biogen's Supply Chain Risk Technology

Technology can help support decision-making, especially in light of the plethora of global events that affect supply chains. For instance, Biogen's Global Security Operations Center (GSOC) in Cambridge, Massachusetts, is an international desk that oversees multiple sites worldwide. A room has multiple television screens and analysts, several cameras, geographic maps of the world, and analytics screens showing global events. The center is staffed by four to five dedicated analysts who monitor social media and global events as well as facilities' security cameras and notifications. The goal of the GSOC is to identify events that could affect Biogen and its employees who are traveling around the world.

The core functions of the GSOC involve synthesizing several systems: physical security systems, integrated access control systems for 26 facilities supported by 1,500 cameras, and global supplier risk programs. For clinical trials, Biogen uses the Resilinc system to show trial sites worldwide and the specific trials going on in each site. This kind of tracking can help alleviate issues when disaster strikes.

For instance, after Hurricane Maria in 2017, there was a shortage of saline bags in Puerto Rico. The executive vice president of clinical research asked whether the company could have known ahead of time which clinical trial sites were using certain ancillary items. Moreover, could the company have understood which items were on low supply, and who produces them?

After this event, the system was revised to predict where and when shortages of items such as saline bags will occur. In addition, GPS technology can track products and map inventory levels for both commercial and clinical trial items. This ensures that shelf lives are not exceeded and that material can be re-dispositioned if it is held up in the supply chain. Individuals who work in the GSOC also have defined operating procedures for alerting key individuals in the organization when an event occurs, aided by technologies that facilitate quick communication links.

This chapter captures important insights on the flow of information, the importance of conveying information in real time during a time of risk, and the importance of freeing up financial flows in the supply chain. We explored digital dexterity and how organizations can work toward creating it. In the next chapter, we continue our discussion of information flows and examine key barriers that may prevent the free flow of energy along the supply chain.

CHAPTER SIX

Electrical Current

The Pulse Center is about having the right information, the right parts and the right deliveries available at the right time. And not all information needs to be broadcast in real time. It depends on what different people need to know, and when they need it.

Mircin Fic, Former Director of Real Time, Flex

You might observe when you walk by a nursing station or ICU in a hospital, that two or three individuals may be managing 30 or 40 patients. Each patient has a pulse, and the nurses monitor all the patients by exception. When the pulse goes wrong, they react. In a similar way, organizations need a centralized monitoring center to manage supply chains by exception, not to monitor everything that is going well. Our observation is that generally speaking, 98 percent of operations in supply chains run well. We need to focus on the two percent that go wrong. In other words, supply chains need humans and software that enable people to make decisions in real time for the two percent of issues that go wrong to improve the effectiveness and efficiency of the supply chain.

This observation reflects the important nature of human-machine interaction and of designing supply chains with information that flows to the right people. Useful information must flow cleanly between parties in the same supply chain, allowing them to collaborate instantaneously. Information flows allow material to move more quickly and allow a quick response to problems. Simply put, a product-industry supply chain is about material in motion. The goal is to move raw material in stages through finished goods as fast as possible. If it is not moving, it is inventory.

Speed is the theory of everything, and supply chain is all about time – weeks, hours, minutes. If supply chains are defined by time, and how efficiently material moves and cost is accumulated are measured using digital tools, it is possible to assess how much better a company can perform. To ensure the flow of material, information about that material must flow. When managers know what is happening with product material and how it is moving through the chain, they are ready to "defrag" their supply chain and reduce the barriers where material gets stuck. Such barriers are like eddies in a river, where debris, sticks, leaves, and trash accumulate. In the supply chain, this debris includes stockrooms full of large stashes of material, obsolete and excess inventory, expired or out-of-date inventory, and warehouses that do not track material availability. This brings us to an important physical law:

Electric current is the ratio of charge and time.

A series circuit is a circuit in which resistors are arranged in a chain, so the current follows a single path. The nodes in a supply chain are like resistors in a circuit. Each upstream action has an impact downstream. Likewise, a disruption in a supply chain upstream has an impact on supply chain flow downstream. To ensure that all entities are aware simultaneously of what is going on, people need to flow together in their decision-making and not work at odds with each other.

In supply chains, fuzzy areas may change on a daily or hourly basis. In such situations, too much information can actually drag people down and prevent them from making a clearly thought-out decision. This is a fine line. Data is a distraction if people are not defragging and cleaning information to get a clear vision of what they want to accomplish. Similarly, situational intelligence is important; when people are moving quickly, they have to be constantly scanning ahead, reacting to situations that arise, and using available data to make split-second decisions. This hyper awareness of incoming data requires important human interaction. This topic is treated in some depth in this chapter.

At Flex, visibility in supply chains was paramount, based on the assumption that you cannot fix what you cannot see. A complex supply chain will never run without some conflict creating a point of decision. For example, a flight may be delayed or a port closed, and action needs to be taken to redirect the circuit – i.e., the flow of the goods – to optimize its time of arrival. Thus, visibility is an a priori condition to supply chain effectiveness. This simple concept is very difficult to anticipate and execute on a day-to-day basis. Lack of visibility prevents the current from running through the desired circuit. Instead, the current may disperse among multiple circuits, leading to a short circuit or the lack of a circuit altogether and no power being transmitted to the desired location.

Unfortunately, most of our supply chains are completely misaligned. This is because most supply chain designs are extremely clunky, making them ill-suited to uncertainty, random events, spikes and lulls in demand, and unexplained behaviors that seem to come out of nowhere. When this happens, buyers, planners, and expeditors spend most of their 12-hour days fighting fires. They are rushing orders or on the phone with suppliers, begging and pleading with them to expedite or postpone a shipment or cancel an order. Interventions like this often occur daily or hourly and can shift in the same day. These problems are not caused by the random events themselves but by supply chains that have not been vaccinated against disruptions and changes in demand and supply. Importantly, immunizing the supply chain begins with demand sensing.

Data and information flow are critical to creating velocity of action and decision-making. Resistance layers often form between companies, which prevent information from flowing seamlessly to key managers. These layers may include firewalls to ensure cybersecurity mandates are followed or restrictions on the size of data files exchanged between companies. Regulatory and legal policies also may interfere with the free flow of data. However, as information is allowed to flow more fluidly between enterprises, velocity and performance benefits will increase.

As we discussed in chapter 5, an important component of digital dexterity is known as a *hinge factor*: the mental agility to respond to and know what to do with data as it flows into one's consciousness. Even as systems evolve to create alerts, identify events, and perhaps even predict them, individuals still must know how to act based on the information presented.

Let us take an historical example, the US Civil War Battle of Gettysburg, and what happened when individual commanders had information that they failed to act on. Confederate General James Longstreet knew the physical landscape and planned to create an envelope around the backside of the opposing force. However, he delayed the offensive on the battle's second day to coordinate his forces, a move that his detractors would later argue allowed Union General George Meade to become more prepared for the Confederate attack. This single decision swung the outcome of the Gettysburg battle and allowed the Union army to win. (This is not the only example; global military history is rife with examples demonstrating that a leader's ability to act (or failure to act) on intelligence determines whether battles are won or lost.)

Having intelligence is not the same as choosing to act on it, and individuals who hesitate to act on data and intelligence can often "lose the moment." For example, the ability to understand patterns that have an impact on forecasts can determine retail winners and losers for a Black Friday sale. If retail planners have sales forecasts in which they are confident but fail to stock inventory in anticipation of the forecasts, then sales will be lost.

History also provides many examples of how progress can be halted by a singular lack of intelligence. In *A World Lit Only by Fire*,[1] William Manchester writes about the pit the world entered when religious dogma shut down progressive thinking. Manchester recounts how detailed observation and data gathering by Michelangelo and Galileo led to revolutionary insights into the physical world. Michelangelo performed autopsies to better understand human muscular and skeletal structure, which led to his lifelike sculptures and paintings. Galileo observed the movements of the sun, stars, and moon to deduce that the Earth was indeed not the center of the universe, contrary to thinking at the time. These visionaries turned around an entire age of ignorance at a time when even basic territorial maps did not exist. People who left their villages generally never returned, as there were no maps to help them find their way back. Visitors to small villages were generally viewed with distrust, and people seldom went outside their rural circles to find out what was going on in the world. Shifts in kingdoms, leadership, the church, and other is-sues were generally unknown, as no news traveled beyond the cities.

Amazingly, a similar thing is happening today: employees of an organization defined by silos are destined to remain ignorant of the conditions that affect other functional areas, customers, suppliers, and technologies. There is a solution: digital toolboxes, which allow employees to visualize the full scope of events oc-curring in their supply chain. Digital intelligence provides the ability to plan and act on events that are outside of immediate view but nevertheless critical to organizational success.

Several stories about "human in the loop" thinking have ap-peared in the media. But where should humans be placed in the supply chain decision-making loop? For instance, bots are used to order pens on a weekly basis. If ordering and supply systems are automated and talking to one another, and they can self-adjust to differences in lead time and availability, human intervention does not seem necessary. But if a relationship issue arises, such as a supplier complaining that the system is not paying on time, humans must be part of the discussion that ensues. The need for human judgment is important because this relates to the ini-tial conditions in which systems are required to establish them-selves. Leaders must consider not only what can be automated safely and securely but also where humans should come in to adjust systems if they spiral out of control and the initial param-eters need to be reset.

Dr. Bejan observed the second law of thermodynamics, which describes irreversibility in nature. Irreversibility refers to a one-way flow, like water over a dam or under a bridge. Similarly, once information has been conveyed to parties in a supply chain, it is in a sense irreversible. If the information is not correct or not trusted, then another irreversible action occurs: people will no longer trust the data or will not use it in the future for making decisions. Thus, establishing data quality and governance is a critical component of information flows in supply chains.

Emerging technologies will certainly provide ways to address concerns related to securing information and to ensure that it gets to the right people without being derailed or hacked. One of the most promising technologies in this area is blockchain, which enables flow while eliminating transaction friction. Transaction friction is eliminated between layers of the buyer-seller relationship, while keeping intact the policies of the uniform commercial code that drive business law and commerce. Companies enter a "private" supply chain, into which only trusted members are allowed. In private blockchain networks, key information can be exchanged freely, and all members of the network can see relevant information in real time. Often you do not want all members in a blockchain to see the information; you want them to see only information that pertains to them. It is possible to do that through cryptography such as zero knowledge proofs.

Blockchain instills a unique form of demand planning that ensures that multiple layers of material requirements planning (MRP) systems – purchase orders, invoices, and receiving – are eliminated. These procurement activities consume an inordinate amount of work and effort: buyers and administrators must track down requisitions to match invoices and purchase orders, ensure they are contract-compliant, and perform myriad other wasteful business-to-business trade activities. Blockchain removes the friction associated with all the forecasting, planning, ordering, receiving, invoicing, and acknowledging activities. A legal agreement known as a *smart contract* cements the commercial terms, creating trust between parties and automating transactions. Thus the business "circuit" is opened for the free flow of electricity (data) between parties.

Operational supply chain performance is dramatically improved by using data as fuel for speed in bringing deep insights and accelerating movement. Other technologies for reducing information friction are under development. For example, the Clear Metal continuous delivery experience (CDX) platform is founded on a feedback loop that constantly learns, adjusts, and gets smarter to provide accurate data. Flow improvements resulting from integrating supply chain partners and eliminating layers of traditional communication can also facilitate movement. Machine-to-machine – or more appropriately, app-to-app – communications, which operate without humans, are becoming much more prevalent, and free flow of information between machines will be much faster, in general, than human interaction and processing. A machine does not wait for the boss to come back from lunch or vacation. It operates by rules embedded in algorithms and automatically handles linkages in the supply chain.

Environmental sensing algorithms detect critical changes in an ecosystem or network. As information flow between organizations and machines increases, environmental sensing in the network will detect shifts in operating conditions, ensuring that supply and demand peaks and valleys are communicated in real time. The environmental network sensing process is similar to the way the body's immune system recognizes invading viruses and harmful biota.

During March, April, and May 2020, anyone taking a trip to the grocery store was baffled to find some aisles were completely and starkly bare. As mentioned in an earlier chapter, fears of scarcity led people to hoard their first and immediate needs: hand sanitizer, toilet paper, meat and protein, cleansers, baby diapers, and paper towels. For these products, demand had always been relatively stable and subject to only minor variations in demand. None of the industries anticipated or sensed that the general population would suddenly produce a surge of demand for these supplies. Even though in many cases there was 30 days of supply in the channel for most of these grocery store items, the sudden rush depleted these inventories in a matter of one or two weeks. The inability of these enterprises to sense that demand would spike due to the fear of COVID and shelter at home led to the shortages.

The second component of environmental sensing is the ability to rapidly scale production up or down based on the demand signal. The consumer goods company Procter & Gamble (P&G) developed a demand-sensing algorithm years ago that was quick to detect even a minor decrease or uptick in demand and instantaneously communicate that information down the supply chain to distributors, manufacturing sites, and suppliers. In fact, even in the midst of COVID, Bounty brand paper towels, manu-factured by P&G, were frequently on the shelf. That is clear evi-dence of the demand signal at work.

If we agree that speed is critical to supply chains, then visi-bility is improved when entities are aligned like a series circuit. However, visibility must also be accompanied by guidelines that allow organizations in the supply chain to interact, resolve conflicts, and cope with new information that the system is not trained to deal with. Most machine learning systems have a training dataset that drives algorithms; although these are learn-ing algorithms, new information that it is not trained to deal with may arise. This is similar to the idea of a physician's scope of practice discussed in chapter 2. However, the criteria for estab-lishing scopes of practice are not always well-defined in sup-ply chains, and machine learning systems are likely to become confused when their scope is not clearly defined. Some machine learning solutions utilize unsupervised learning, where the machine works on its own to discover patterns and information that were previously undetected.

A good example here has to do with provenance, which means the origin of where something came from. Safe milk guidelines are based on a specific set of philosophies. A milk supplier's guiding philosophy is that safe milk is important. However, ensuring that a business lives up to its philosophy involves multiple and often very complex considerations related to employees, process, and technology. A milk supplier must consider: What organizations do I join? What rules do I establish for my company that match my underlying philosophy? How is my facility laid out to comply with guidelines for safe handling? How do I train my employees in safe milk handling procedures? What am I feeding the cows? Which refrigerated trucks and warehouses are in proximity to the customer's point of consumption? Clearly, milk cannot travel across the desert in an unrefrigerated container because it will go sour. Thus, multiple layers of compliance are required to uphold a provenance philosophy, and the scope of practice is carefully defined by the FDA, or its equivalent in other countries, on how to safely handle the production and distribution of milk.

Another good example is a soccer or football coach, who walks into the locker room on game day with a plan. But the coach's strategies are largely situational; he or she must adapt the game to what the other coach is doing. The coach must constantly scan and react to what is happening on the field: what is the other team deploying in the last half? The importance of such situational planning is critical for managing supply chains. In this case, data is the basis for decision-making and adaptation to the environment, much like the work done in complex network analysis. Physics determines certain principles that demand rigidity for planning, but a situation mindset is needed to be successful. The importance of timing, quick decision-making, and information flow brings us to another important physical law: power.

Electric Power and Time

The physical law of electrical power is a good metaphor for understanding how decision-making flows from data.

> Electrical power is the rate, per unit time, at which electrical energy is transferred by an electric circuit. It is the rate of doing work.
>
> $W = VQ/t$
>
> Where
>
> W = watts (unit of power)
>
> V = volts
>
> Q = charge (coulombs)
>
> T = time

> One watt is the rate at which work is done when a current of one ampere flows through a network that has an electrical potential difference of one volt.

Electrical power increases when the time during which the electrical energy is applied is reduced. In the context of this law, power can be increased if one increases the force applied to an object. However, the same electrical force, applied in the same quantity for a shorter period of time, increases the overall power of the system.

When we think of electrical power, we are attracted to the notion of power or force in motion. This is a useful context for discussion of another critical component of how data flows through supply chains. Electrical current provides a useful metaphor for visualizing how information flows between people and how individuals can work together in a supply chain to drive results. This is perhaps an overly simplistic metaphor, but it is a powerful one nevertheless. If one begins with the premise that speed of transmission of data can improve the quality and velocity of decision-making, a combination of machine and human decision-making approaches can be applied to supply chains and produce incredible outcomes.

In previous chapters, we described how the Pulse worked at Flex. To review, the Pulse is a vehicle for instantaneously showing the real-time status of material in every stage of its complex supply chains. The data were pulled from multiple systems and broadcast instantaneously, not only to a centralized control tower but to hundreds of thousands of smartphones. To this end, users could quickly determine the status of an order, a disruption, or of inventory in the system. In this case, it is clear that the ability to visualize information through effective human-machine interfaces drives performance. Less importance is placed on the specific performance metrics, but being able to see the live feed of data on a supply chain drives humans to act more decisively and with greater confidence in these decisions. Good decisions cannot be made without good data.

What types of data are shown in the Flex Pulse? Examples include current lead-times, minimum order quantities, inventory levels, inbound shipment arrival times, and purchase order execution signals. This information is linked to decisions made by many people today.

"We have too many diverse software systems – they're siloed and can't interact," many executives complain. However, the key to improving data flow and increasing the current of data is to understand and define the specific types of data required, and what they are being used for. A learning algorithm, by overseeing human decisions, can learn to respond to disruptive events autonomously, for example, increasing a minimum order quantity or notifying a distributor that material is now available.

Thus, the first signal in the chain can be linked by algorithms to create notifications through APIs to other software systems that control other parts of the supply chain. Humans can still stay in the loop, perhaps in the "pole position" of making the call to increase buffers when a risk is identified. But other activities can occur without humans having to make the call, as machines will eventually start to learn by observing human behaviors. By combining human skills with the right machine recognition technologies, the electrical flows of event monitoring and reaction can become uninhibited and quicker to respond.

The Demand Sensing Problem

Some argue not only that inventory is necessary for supply chains but that more inventory is better. This belief has become particularly popular in the post-COVID era. The media, Congress, and others have lamented that just-in-time has failed and that large stockpiles of inventory should be carried by the federal government and the private sector to guard against emergencies. Indeed, without available inventory, an enterprise cannot build a product or ship a finished product to a customer. It only takes one missing component in a bill of materials to shut down an entire supply chain. So to qualify the rule that "greater velocity is better" in the physics of supply chains, we note that movement of material should occur at maximum efficiency for the purpose at hand.

For example, the parts to produce the product and the time to source them from suppliers should be optimized so that the product is produced immediately after all the parts arrive, and the product should be shipped upon completion. To make this happen, however, the demand system has to be extremely observant in detecting even minor changes in demand levels. This is called *demand sensing*. When there are indicators that something is about to go wrong – that demand will spike or drop suddenly – the production system needs to increase power, much like an electrical circuit being switched on.

These principles started the just-in-time revolution pioneered by Toyota and others in Japan[2] and were copied extensively by companies worldwide from 1980 to today. Movement was also proven by continuous flow manufacturing in the 1970s and by Dell's cash-optimized supply chain in the 1980s and 1990s.[3] In the 2000s, demand sensing was further optimized by Amazon's flywheel.[4] Just in time has received plenty of criticism during COVID, but its principles remain intact, as the disruptions that occurred had nothing to do with organizations who employed lean systems.

Demand sensing represents the real promise of artificial intelligence and machine-based learning in managing supply chains. The media has focused on the promise of autonomous trucks. In our opinion, due to the regulatory climate and instability of the technology, these trucks will not be on the road for at least 10 years. However, the true magic of artificial intelligence in the supply chain will occur with the compression of time and business. Supply chain speed of action will move inventory more quickly and thus reduce working capital on the balance sheet. As companies compress the white space between events, when nothing is happening, transactions occur more quickly and with greater visibility. Moreover, the flow of data occurs instantaneously, rather than requiring human intervention and decision-making at each stage.

One of the most important forms of demand sensing will come from information transmitted by inanimate objects, or what is known as *the edge*. This idea represents a radical departure from current technology, but it is also consistent with the physical observation that trees, rocks, and landscapes change over time. The edge refers to a business scenario in which sensors are increasingly being attached to objects, whether they are trucks, inventory, pallets, electrical systems, thermometers, or other objects. Eventually, most inanimate objects will have sensors that will provide information from the edge of the network. All these technologies communicate information from inanimate objects back to the center, much as it happened in the science fiction film *Terminator 3: Rise of the Machines*.

Every device is getting smarter. Eventually, all homes will be installed with smart devices, including the water meter, the refrigerator, the stove, the electrical system, and the thermostat. We will also likely see boxes and shipments with sensors that self-select the trucks that will pick them up and take them to their destination. These digital supply chains will dominate all others because they can holistically create insights into upstream and downstream conditions, allowing managers to see all, using data from the edge combined with demand-sensing data.

As people work more from home in a post-COVID world, we will likely see holograms replacing people meeting face-to-face. Virtual white boards and maps will enable new levels of collaboration. Sensors will also be used to alert managers to shipment status and allow expediting. For example, a manager will be able to see where their shipment is – perhaps sitting at a port in Hong Kong – and the system may connect that box to a container that is leaving one day earlier than scheduled. A robot picks up the box and puts it in the container. Inanimate objects are now communicating with one another, and every digital generation will become more intelligent. This development will dramatically increase the velocity of supply chains and take humans out of the equation for any decisions driven by a common objective: to speed up moving materials. People will be needed, but machines can often make decisions without bias or hesitation.

Consider that throughout history, time and again, pauses in human decision-making have been the major cause of lost battles. We are again reminded of General George McClellan's foolish decisions at Antietam, where, in possession of Robert E. Lee's entire war strategy, he did nothing with the information. He could have divided the enemy, then destroyed them at his leisure, putting an end to the Civil War. And yet, according to Eric Durschmied, "he did nothing, performed no reconnaissance, and issued no orders, and not a single one of his commanders dared to tell him to do so."[5]

Consider an example where a supply chain planner perceives that lead times have shortened, that a supplier has more material available, and that a risk has been mitigated. Instead of acting immediately, this planner may need a manager's approval before adjusting the memorandum of understanding and lead time in the system. But what if the person's direct manager is sick or traveling and is not available for a week or more? Until notified, the planner sits on the information or escalates the decision to someone else, who is also tied up. Thirty days or more may go by before approval for the decision eventually occurs, during which time inventory has been sitting, losing value, in a distribution center or warehouse. Politics have gotten in the way of simple material flow decisions. The takeaway is that organizations must stay true to the physics of supply chain and remain practical by focusing on the core elements of speed, distance, flow, and weight.

Too much data can also cause a slowdown, and having a lot of data does not speed up decision-making. We have heard many executives complain, "I have too much data and can't make a decision, as I don't know what to look for." It is critical to understand what data are important and ensure that data will flow without friction and resistance to the nodes in the supply chain that have autonomous decision-making authority, enabled by artificial intelligence. One way to improve data flow is to shed light on it, which will expose people to what is going on. Increasing visibility and automating decisions that increase flow is one way to break down silos that delay decision-making. In this sense, freeing up data unleashes the electrical power that will run the supply chain and make it run faster.

It is important to keep in mind that a loss of power almost always occurs in an electrical current. For instance, as electrons move through a wire during magnetic induction, some of those electrons are diverted from a straight path through the wire. This is accompanied with something like vibrations of the molecular structure of the wire, which leads to heat dissipation and heat radiation, or loss of power.

Similarly, data used to support supply chain decisions will not be perfect, and there will be some loss of fidelity. When someone notices that the data is really bad, and shines a light on it, somebody is ultimately responsible for that data. Ideally, that person quickly steps up, takes accountability for it, and works to fix the problem. Executives who consider these scenarios suddenly understand the true impact that freeing up data in their organizations will have on their organizations and are doing something about it.

Supply chain management functions are beginning to view data from a much broader perspective; some even refer to it as the new oil. C-level management has expressed increased expectations that data analytics will yield continual cost and process improvement resulting from the increased use of data-driven business decisions. The creation of a data asset management strategy to enable improved supply chain management has become one of the more prevalent functional views.

Marketing has been using data analytics for some time. However, supply chain managers are only now beginning to realize the potential impact of improved analytical insight for supply chain decisions, particularly in light of demands for quicker next-day delivery, lower working capital, and complex supply chains. This spans several areas, including making procurement, materials management, customer order fulfillment, and assortment and stocking more integral to an enterprise data asset management strategy. The biggest problem to overcome is the mindset that we can be digitally free when we are away from work but must conform to the old IT systems that bind us at work – especially in the form of tired Excel files.

Becoming a Digital Native at Work: A Culture of Action (Velocity)

Becoming attuned to the world of digitization will not be unfamiliar to most of us. As Hans Melotte, chief procurement officer at Starbucks, once noted, everyone needs to digitize their supply chains.

"From 5 p.m. to 9 a.m., I am a digital native," Melotte said. "I use my mobile phone to make decisions, order products, navigate my way home and multiple other tasks. But at 9 a.m., I am back at the office, and I am back in the world of Excel spreadsheets, with no visibility into what is happening in my supply chain. We need to become digital natives at work, not just at home."

Creating a culture for visibility is a key component of change. This involves delegating authority, including assigning employees to roles associated with information velocity, who know how to act on it quickly. Tolerance of failure is an important component because quick action in the face of uncertainty is always a risk. However, managers should encourage their team to take calculated risks based on information and to act quickly. At Flex, the challenge was to make sure 140,000 people were utilizing information in a more productive way to make decisions. The idea, of course, is not for everyone to look at all the data all the time, but for people to look at the right data at the right time.

An important caveat to ensuring that data improves decisions is when its flow between people in organizations speeds up. There is a fine line between making a fast decision and a fast decision that is also a good decision.

A recent study by McKinsey suggests that not all organizations currently make appropriate decisions in the face of urgency.[6] Organizations that eliminate the trade-off in decision-making between velocity (How fast was the decision made and executed?) and quality (How good was the decision?) see better financial results and higher growth rates and returns from their decisions. This was the case across three types of decisions: "big-bet" strategic decisions, cross-cutting middle management decisions, and delegated or tactical decisions. Decision-makers who can make fast, high-quality decisions had several supportive organizational policies in place. This included the ability to query data and disconfirm initial hypotheses quickly, standard processes for decision-making meetings that everyone followed, and the ability to be biased toward action and allowing people to fail safely. These policies create the right environment for people to look at data, interpret it, and make a quick decision.

Overcoming Obstacles: Finance, IT, and Legal Issues

Many companies we speak with are hesitant to act on the policies outlined above because they are unable to construct an effective business case for data transparency and rapid decision-making. "What's the ROI?[7]" is a common question. The key is to establish the business case not on market share, but through velocity of material and decision-making, enabling managers to take rapid actions in the face of uncertainty using the most up-to-date information. There is always the possibility of wrong decisions, but the benefits of velocity often supersede the costs.

Legal counsel in organizations will argue that privacy and security are often a concern. There is no arguing against this point of view; it is an extension of risk management that every legal counsel will push for. To address this issue, leaders must take care to establish the right governance structure. This structure should be guided by the Law of Transparency: people need access to information that ensures they can react and thereby improve supply chain outcomes. Leaders should also set appropriate "firewalls" between individuals so as not to violate legal connectivity policies.

Another concern has to do with releasing validated data. Rob Handfield recently attended a meeting in which there was a discussion on this topic in the pharmaceutical sector. Specifically, executives debated whether data from manufacturing and material handling that is validated using good manufacturing processes (GMP) could be shared with partners if it has not been fully vetted? Let us consider several possible responses. First, the FDA and other agencies require GMP data only for specific reporting applications. Second, demand forecasts and production/inventory data are not GMP-regulated and thus are not subject to this validation argument. Third, GMP data is typically one of the most important data types required by quality assurance specialists but is often not required for making supply chain shipping decisions. Thus, there is no reason why forecast and inventory data cannot be shared among partners.

CIOs are also concerned about data security. At Flex, most of the information on the Pulse was new data that was not currently within the four walls of the organization. That made the argument a lot easier, since the supply chain team did not wish to "violate the CIO's security stack." Pulling internal data and hosting it on a cloud server where it can be shared will not expose the organization to cybersecurity risks, since hackers will not have structural access to the organization's data. In this sense, creating a real-time supply chain involves hosting only data that is required to operate the supply chain and can be shared with key supply chain partners. When data is shared outside the walls of the organization, it may be necessary to encrypt it. (There is some interesting research being done on homomorphic encryption at MIT and other places. This allows organizations to share data and retain complete control over who can access or perform analysis on it at a granular level, and have auditability of the process.) These considerations render the real-time supply chain easier to execute and can overcome concerns regarding data sharing leading to cybersecurity risks.

Tom Linton has noted that you cannot let IT and the CIO control your destiny. Supply chain executives have to take control of this factor. CIOs will throw "systems jargon" at you. Acting to control your destiny means finding a way around these arguments to drive real-time visibility of information required to operate your supply chain more efficiently.

Another excellent example of an organization that sought to "free the data" is Merck KGA. Rob Handfield spoke with Alessandro DeLuca, CIO of Merck KGA. DeLuca worked for 25 years in supply chain, including five years with P&G as it deployed its demand-sensing algorithms to project demand from consumers all the way into the supply chain through a demand signal. When his CEO asked him to become the CIO, he recalled, "I don't know anything about IT. But my boss told me that is exactly why he wants me to be the CIO – so I could be more impactful on the business."

DeLuca is a firm believer in the industry-wide shift toward automated supply chains, but also believes that jobs change through a process called *artificial intelligence augmentation*. DeLuca argues that artificial intelligence can augment the jobs of supply chain planners and reduce often tedious and repetitive work. The technology is on a platform supported by Aera, which allows supply chain employees to see a real-time view of global supply and demand activity. Supply chain data is captured from dozens of repositories and ERP systems and transferred to the cloud infrastructure on Amazon Web Services (AWS). Machine learning algorithms analyze the data and determine whether and when to adjust product supply or demand forecasts. These algorithms factor in external data such as weather, natural disasters, trends in patient health, and in some cases, pharmacy expansion plans. So these planners use the technology but must be retrained to think more like supply chain architects.

In the long term, DeLuca said, "We are going to have a single source of truth, around P&L, shortages, working capital and other key metrics. The demand planner and the general manager will be able to access the same kind of information, which will drive a lot of change management. Technology is the easy part; mindset is, however, very hard to change."

Merck KGA's movement toward supply chain professionals having a greater say about the transparency of data in enterprise systems is not unique. A recent study[8] shows an increased involvement of supply chain management personnel on enterprise data governance committees seeking to "free the data." In some cases, supply chain executives are taking the lead in driving analytics for the enterprise. Data governance committees are primarily focused on data asset management, which comprises four key categories:

1 **Data quality and governance**. Timely, complete, accurate, and relevant data governed by a set of processes and rules that validate the sources of data (both internal and external), perform data audits, and determine when data should no longer be used in analysis, etc.
2 **Data catalogs**. Consistent data descriptions (data dictionaries) and tagging, which provide a means of repeatable retrieval of data assets for cleaning, organizing, and analysis
3 **Uniform data accessibility**. Standardized data asset repositories for both external and internal real-time sources of data
4 **Analytics**. Real-time predictive and prescriptive analytics operating with standardized analytic and artificial intelligence tools

Digitization of supply chain processes simply cannot occur without an active data quality and governance program that addresses all internal and external data sources. Development of all "higher-order" analytics projects, including artificial intelligence, internet of things, blockchain, and contract automation all depend on an effective data quality and governance foundation.

The need for security creates many concerns, especially as organizations become more risk averse when it comes to openly sharing data.

Dark Clouds over the Cloud

Information flows, particularly those involving open sharing of information, rely to a large extent on cloud technology, which allows large datasets and information to be exchanged in a virtual environment. While many executives were hesitant to enter the cloud environment five years ago due to security concerns, these concerns were rapidly overcome. Nowadays, most organizations and supply chains employ publicly available cloud services such as AWS, Microsoft Azure, Google Cloud, Salesforce, IBM Cloud, and Oracle Cloud. However, recent discussions with executives working in supply chains reveal that there may be a pull-back from this collaborative cloud environment. People are hesitating to jump into the cloud and are pulling back to the old enterprise software model. There are four primary reasons for this hesitation to put data into the cloud:

1 **Security (especially cybersecurity) and data privacy**. Accessibility versus security is an issue everyone faces. An increasing number of organizations rely on internet of things and mobile devices designed to provide the maximum level of accessibility and data availability anywhere they need it, at any time.[9] In addition, many companies have outsourced security. However, with an increasing number of issues around targeted cyberattacks, such as the ransomware incident that occurred around Merck's supply chain, more companies are moving to handle cybersecurity inside their organizations because they view it as a core security issue. Many internal security concerns are handled in an ad hoc manner, producing a Frankenstein system of jerry-rigging fixes. In short, the trend toward internal cybersecurity centers is ramping up, creating a hodgepodge of data security standards.

2 **Industry compliance concerns.** A host of new industry compliance standards is emerging. Many of these are industry specific, including Federal Risk and Authorization Management Program (FedRAMP), Payment Card Industry (PCI),

Health Insurance Portability and Accountability (HIPAA), GMP, and FDA. They are rooted in antiquated models of running software that must comply with operational guidelines. These old standards do not operate well in a cloud-based environment, and the rules for operating in a cloud-based environment are still being written.

3 **Points of control.** In many enterprises, the IT function does not want to lose control over how it does business. In supply chains, people want transaction response time to occur in milliseconds and they want to control that response time. EDI transactions can take seconds to minutes due to batch processing, but for inventory control, customer expectations regarding response time are key. In short, people believe they need control and that sending their data to the cloud means losing that control.

4 **Order management software.** Back-office monitoring of point-of-sale terminals is being used on the back end to complete order fulfillment and order-balancing planning activities. This requires heavy customization as well as a strong data backbone for robust order management system analysis. Customization of data outputs is often difficult and clunky to achieve when data is being run through a continuous integration/continuous delivery (CI/CD) data pipeline.[10] Users do not feel comfortable deploying code to run somewhere in the cloud but want to know where things should happen as they should. However, infrastructure as code could possibly address this issue and would help to reduce manual configuration, which is resource intensive, error prone, and costly. Users could manage the desired state of the tech infrastructure using configuration files and determine the security configuration and governance before the infrastructure is deployed in the cloud.

Within the next five years, organizations can look forward to many emerging supply chain technologies, including the following:

- **Interfaces between systems**. There remain significant challenges to understanding the interface between supply chain systems and developing predictive analytics. The application of artificial intelligence is often lauded as critical, but it is not well understood yet. There may be some early wins that are glaringly obvious (e.g., tracking the value of shipments). But more subtle applications exist that are more impactful, and they may be held back because they must traverse multiple dispersed systems. Supply chain organizations need to work closely with developers to identify problems for which emerging technologies can be applied, work through the data challenges, and learn how to apply data science to predict potential or current problems. Early identification of risks allows decision-makers to act quickly. As we have seen during the COVID crisis, buying time after a disaster is not possible, and acting quickly to acquire materials before they are depleted is critical.
- **Blockchain**. Blockchain will continue to be important, although people are going through blockchain fatigue at the moment. The primary strength and potential for blockchain is its distributed application. Questions remain about the current state of the blockchain industry, and about what reasonable paths exist for leveraging blockchain around a defined business case.
- **Self-correcting supply chains.** Companies have made great strides in deploying artificial intelligence and data science, but they still have a limited ability to correct the flow of human errors that often occurs in order-fulfillment processes.

How can organizations build the "self-correcting" supply chain? How can artificial intelligence establish corrective actions for a customer? What patterns and building blocks will kick-start self-correction? What is the level of trust from a human and organizational perspective? Can we let people know what the options are, observe their decision-making, and then automate it? These are fundamental questions for emerging technology applications.

How Agile Is Supply Chain Data?

In the remainder of the chapter, we share details from a recent report on data governance and quality conducted by the Supply Chain Resource Cooperative in conjunction with the business software company IValua.[11]

Businesses are making progress in improving data quality and governance in their supply chains – but slowly. Perhaps this is because many executives are not aware of the problem. Indeed, executives often complain about data overload, failing to recognize that the first step is to identify the critical data they need. Executives report that they believe the quality of the data being used in the supply chain is improving, with 28 percent rating their data quality as good, and nine percent as excellent (see figure 6.1).

Multiple factors may explain this improvement, but the most important may be the increased recognition of supplier risk. Organizations that have experienced significant supply chain disruptions in the last two years now recognize that giving their suppliers access to their master data is key to mapping their supply chains and understanding sources of risk. Emerging solutions, such as the one from Elm Analytics,[12] are focused on

FIGURE 6.1. *Data quality*

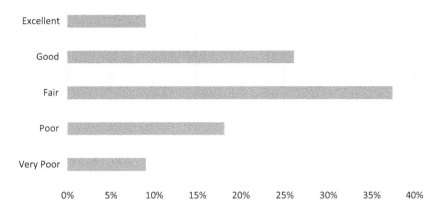

mapping out supply chains in industries such as automotive by engaging suppliers across multiple tiers. Organizations now recognize that although data governance is a grind, it is imperative to improving supplier master data. Major steps for accomplishing this include:

- Standardizing and automating the process of supplier data capture and maintenance
- Cleansing and enriching existing and new data, and harmonizing it across systems
- Capturing additional supplier details through forms, assessments, or surveys to drive more complete information, improve compliance, manage risk, and enable communication
- Providing an enterprise view of clear, comprehensive, and accurate supplier information

To continue to improve supplier data, leaders must recognize what a cleansed supplier database will look like, as depicted in table 6.1:

TABLE 6.1. *Migrating to a clean supplier database*

From	To
Multiple supplier numbers for the same supplier	One supplier number for each supplier
Fragmented supplier management	Company common supplier on-boarding and lifecycle management solution
Supplier profile data not accessible to the supplier	Profile data accessed and managed by supplier
Multiple sources of inconsistent data consolidated into multiple data warehouses	One source of core business data for consistent, trusted reporting and analysis in one data warehouse
No definition for data leadership	One definition of core business data and clear business ownership
Entity-driven master data decisions and designs	Company-driven program approach

In 2019, 77 percent of firms rated their overall data quality as fair, good, or excellent, compared to 46 percent for the same classifications in 2018. However, the fact that most executives still rate their data as only fair is evidence that everyone recognizes that a long road lies ahead before data quality is improved.

Many firms' data quality challenges may be due to the fact that organizations continue to acquire and merge with other companies. Any merger results in a period of wandering in the data wilderness, as businesses continue to operate in data silos, using their own ERP systems, materials systems, and financial reporting systems. Pulling these systems together to create analytical insight is a gargantuan task that may take years.

Perhaps because of this recognition, executives are now more aware than ever that data governance is essential for harnessing and getting an ROI from analytics investments. As figure 6.2 shows, the perception that data governance is a necessity is at its

FIGURE 6.2. *Perspectives on data governance*

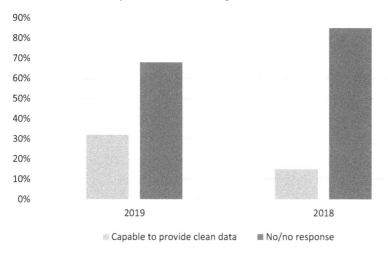

highest level since 2017. Many recognize that access to reliable good-quality data enables their managers to work more effectively, whether in the office or at home. The data suggests that two-thirds of executives recognize that having staff members who can analyze data to make better decisions is important for their organizations to remain competitive.

Proactive and forward-looking leaders recognize the value of putting reliable data in the hands of their staff members and allowing individuals to dive into data and search for answers. However, our study suggests that there is still some reluctance on the part of executives to allow staff to analyze data on their own. Some fear that data analysis may be too difficult for people to handle. Platforms such as Tableau have been around for a while, yet many companies are dragging their heels despite the fact that the rising group of millennials entering the workforce is not afraid to dive in and learn on the fly. The challenge is to organize data interpretation into actionable activities based on an understanding of business processes, thus linking data analysis to sound business knowledge.

Impact of Poor Data on Supply Chain Productivity

Results from the data governance and quality survey show that supply chain managers still spend a large part of their days looking for data. Specifically, 53 percent spend more than 10 percent of their days looking for data that they need for analysis. About nine percent do not even know how much time they spend. A comparison of 2017–19 data suggests that while our ability to find clean data has significantly improved, the data may still lack organization or classification, because the amount of time we spend looking for data has significantly increased. While the amount of time spent looking for data is going up, this may be a function of having more people spend more time working on analytics activity in general.

The results also show that the capability to find clean data improved significantly in 2019, with more than 32 percent of respondents saying they can use the data once they locate it, versus 15 percent in 2018. Efforts to improve data quality are yielding some benefits, although the time required to locate and cleanse data has an impact on productivity.

One area in which organizations have made significant improvements is developing algorithms to create dashboards and control towers for senior executives in procurement and other areas. As noted in the Siemens case study in chapter 5, end-of-quarter reporting used to take several weeks of activity, including pulling data from multiple systems, cleansing it, and putting it into Excel charts. The company has made dramatic improvements in this process, to the point where real-time metrics are calculated with the "click of a mouse."

Creating Data Flows

One emerging issue in supply chain management is data overload. Supply chain managers are weighed down by too much data and too much information intermixed with bad data. We all experience this as we fight to keep our inboxes at a minimum level. Data has weight and can slow things down if it is not put on a diet. This involves identifying essential data in a sea of information. For example, in a bill of material, one or two components may dictate whether or not a product is clear to build in manufacturing. Often, something simple that was late to arrive or in shortage for a season can create a massive revenue miss (e.g., the semiconductor shortage impacting the automotive sector in 2021–2). Systems that highlight the few strategic constraints that drive "clear-to-build" availability make or break a supply chain performance result.

Good data governance is perhaps the most important driver of improved data flow. The second is understanding at a broad level what managers need to understand. If the data is not always perfect, it is important to know whether it is directionally correct and has a margin of error that allows decision-making under uncertainty. This is why visualization of data and use of indicators such as red, yellow, and green to identify trends and patterns are so useful. When users can begin to visualize data, they can quickly begin to make sense of it.

At Flex, 94 applications were connected through its APIs to create visual representation of events in the supply chain. It is difficult to have one solution to solve all problems, so Tom Linton decided to use the best features of every application and link them all through APIs. This also gave the team the ability to update and integrate each piece of information individually and produce a more robust system.

In addition to digital flows, financial flows are an important component of keeping supply chains working, particularly during major crises such as COVID or financial meltdowns. Supply chain financing plays a critical role in ensuring the immunity of supply chains. This is particularly important given the challenging times facing many small-to-medium size suppliers, which are struggling to keep their doors open during one of the biggest economic recessions in recent history.

Liquid Inventory: Improving Financial Flows through Supply Chain Financing

An important illustration of the importance of flows is the gravitational flow of cash as it moves through the supply chain. Cash that is not moving can have devastating effects, particularly for small businesses that do not have a large pool of funds. During the COVID and the economic crises, many of these small-to-medium size enterprises (SMEs) struggled to pay bills when their customers withheld or delayed payments by 90 or 120 days. This had an impact on payments to workers, as well as payments to upstream material suppliers, effectively shutting down their ability to produce orders during a time of economic instability.

However, a new group of companies has sought to restore the natural pull of gravity, restoring financial flows using a strategy called supply chain financing. These supply chain intermediaries have made important contributions to reducing working capital and increasing free cash flow. The Global Supply Chain Finance Forum[13] defines supply chain finance (SCF) as the use of financing and risk mitigation practices to optimize management of the working capital and liquidity invested in supply chain processes and transactions.

SCF is typically applied to open account trade, and it is triggered by supply chain events. Finance providers must have access to information about the company's underlying trade flows, which can be enabled by a technology platform. This kind of finance provides the flow of funds that keeps the supply chain running. Think of it as "liquid inventory," in that it frees up working capital and cash flow so the supply chain does not grind to a halt.

The world of supply chain financing has grown significantly in the last five years. As an asset class, the returns on these capital investments have fallen considerably. On one hand, growth in the SCF industry has increased the appetite of large multinational enterprises (MNEs) to increase their payable timelines; the growth has also provided many smaller suppliers quicker payment on their receivables. Software companies such as SAP and Ariba have made it increasingly easy for SME suppliers to access immediate payment of invoices through "click" buttons available in these systems. In a sense, this has created a race to the bottom, as the basis points (interest rate calculations) associated with supply chain financing have gone lower and lower.

Another big shift in the sector has been the introduction of the Basel III Accord regulations.[14] Prior to this requirement, a bank might lend money to a large retailer such as Walmart at two percent interest, while concurrently lending funds to Sears at a rate of 10 percent due to that company's increased risk. The bank could hold a single capital reserve for losses that would cover both loans.

Since Basel III, however, the lender's reserve has to be aligned with both accounts. In this case, the reserve for Sears might have to be eight times as large as the reserve for Walmart, requiring the bank to set aside significant amounts of capital. This has made it increasingly complex for banks to calculate the right return and to make many of the more risky loans in the ecosystem. Credit risk information is readily available for larger suppliers. But as large companies seek to create financing options for numerous smaller suppliers, banks struggle to calculate the credit risks and assign ratings to these much smaller accounts. This is largely due to the difficulty of finding financial information on smaller companies that are not listed on public stock exchanges.

Let us put this issue in context. Suppose three major MNEs – P&G, Coca-Cola, and Airbus – each have 20,000 suppliers. About 2,500 suppliers, or 10 percent, have credit scores that enable them to access well-priced working capital. This leaves another 17,500 small suppliers, as well as their tier-2 suppliers, that would like to gain access to financing. This is because the MNEs often impose longer payment terms (say, 120 days) on smaller suppliers. Current marketplace/peer-to-peer lending options available to SMEs may be as high as 35 percent per annum, and the amount of financing available may be limited.

Although the risk profile of smaller suppliers is generally high, if they are selling to a large company such as Coca-Cola, which has a superior credit rating, that rating can be leveraged to provide lower-cost financing to the SMEs. If Coca-Cola vets that supplier and introduces the financing program to the SME, the SME will gain access to a finance rate almost equivalent to what Coca-Cola would get. It makes sense that suppliers that receive a lower finance rate would have a lower chance of bankruptcy than a similar-sized company in a similar industry without access to improved financing terms through a large corporate customer.

Extending credit to a larger swath of the supply base would result in significantly lower MNE supplier risk and would enhance the ability of supply chain managers to target higher-risk suppliers, such as diverse and smaller suppliers.

The context of supply chain financing on working capital can be illustrated through an example. Suppose Small and Minority

Enterprise A with $10 million of annual revenue sells products locally to other small businesses, none of which have a focused approach to sourcing, monitoring, coaching, or monitoring their supply chains. Small and Minority Enterprise B has similar revenue, is in the same industry sector, has been in business the same amount of time as SME A, but sells to large MNEs. Although the risk profiles of these two suppliers may appear equivalent, it is reasonable to expect that Small and Minority Enterprise B will fail less often, and there are leading indicators that may help the MNE. In this case, a financial institution providing working capital to Supplier B would have more confidence in their ability to predict the failure of the supplier.

Understanding these indicators could help provide SCF companies with greater insight into their ability to finance SMEs who sell to MNEs. For example, these insights could generate a risk rating for similar smaller suppliers in a specific industry niche and enable greater coverage of the supply base. Distinctions could also be made based on different supplier criteria, including industry sector, sub-sector, size, country of origin, minority-owned, length of relationship (two years or less), and other parameters. Risk ratings could be established based on empirical evidence and create greater access for all parties to assess risk and financing terms for a greater number of suppliers.

The SCF industry is sure to grow in the next five to 10 years as access to working capital becomes critical for organizations to manage extended payment terms in a global supply chain. In the short term, it could also help to keep SMEs afloat, particularly as they face difficulty in maintaining commercial liquidity in the face of revenue shortfalls in a post-COVID recession.

In the next case study, we examine how digital flows can alert companies and provide them with early warning of issues several tiers down in the supply chain.

Case Study 8: Flex's Early Warning Systems Identified COVID Risks[15]

Flex is a large contract manufacturer based in Singapore, with 100 facilities in 30 countries. Some factories are in China,[16] but this number has been declining. Flex's chief supply chain officer, Revathi Advaithi, cut the company's dependence on Chinese supply by half over a five-year period and expanded capacity in other countries, including the United States. Flex's customers have increasingly been demanding regional production networks rather than a single global supply chain from China. But on January 13, 2020, the immediate concern was what was going on in China.

Advaithi had just returned from holiday in India to her home near Flex's US headquarters in San Jose, California, when she was alerted to an event that was probably the most difficult time in her 30-year career. On a call with Francois Barbier, Flex's head of operations, on January 13, she learned that the coronavirus spreading across China showed no sign of abating. The team brought a lot of data and information to a meeting. At that time, rumors were swirling that the Chinese government might order factories to remain closed after the annual New Year holiday, which would lead to an extended interruption in manufacturing. This would have an impact on some of the many products manufactured by Flex for companies such as Google, Fiat Chrysler, HP, Xerox, and Apple, as well as Phillips ventilators.

Barbier had in effect detected the proverbial "canary in a coal mine" and picked up on the fact that something wrong was happening in China. Advaithi's team moved quickly, by first agreeing to order enough PPE (masks, gloves, temperature scanners, and hand sanitizer) for Flex's 50,000 Chinese workers. Two weeks later, with most of China under quarantine, 3 million masks from other regions in Asia had reached Flex's Chinese operations. This early warning sign and subsequent response paid off. In China, Wang Ming, general manager for Flex's Suzhou and Shanghai plants, had kept skeleton crews working throughout the holiday, making semiconductor equipment, telecom gear, CT scanners, and bedside patient monitors for the Chinese market. However, by early February he battled shortages of labor and material, as many of his 5,000 workers could not return to work from holiday visits because of cutoff rail and bus services due to COVID. Recognizing the bottlenecks, he equipped his immediate suppliers with masks, cleaning supplies, and training manuals.

By the end of March, Flex had spent $52 million on coronavirus-related expenses, with the total bill topping $100 million. Flex's leadership immediately began working almost exclusively via Zoom calls. The chief procurement officer, Lynn Torrell, monitored over 16,000 suppliers and more than 1 million items using the Pulse (described earlier in this book), which combined data from Flex's 88 sources. She was able to monitor late deliveries using a feature similar to a car warning system, which provided alerts when something was going wrong. Part of the challenge involved flagging parts originating from China and reconfirming orders with suppliers and customers to ensure that orders were actually being produced and were still needed (i.e., that it was true demand). In some cases, alternative suppliers were found when production dried up in China. Another problem was that many of the components from China traveled to the United States in the belly of passenger jets. Major airlines had canceled more than 1 million flights, and air cargo rates had spiked, so special accommodations had to be made through relationships with airline managers.

The situation became progressively worse as many Chinese suppliers were physically unable to return to factories because of government-ordered quarantines, so inventory had to be located from other operating factories by shifting production needs. Despite having to juggle customer demands, the company never suffered a complete breakdown of its global supply chain. By February 16, more than half of Flex's Chinese workforce was back on the job, but problems were spreading to other Flex factories in Italy and Brazil, requiring the team to apply the same playbook to these affected areas. Flex's global operations continued to recover, and by May 8, the company had eked out a $48 million profit on revenue of $5.5 billion for the first three months of the year.

The Pulse, combined with the early warnings of problems occurring at factories in China in early January, was essential in enabling Flex's effective immunity response to the COVID crisis. Although the company certainly did experience a "sickness" associated with the impact of the pandemic on its supply chain, its ability to monitor materials in real time was a critical component that enabled an effective immune response. With all factories operating and parts availability back to normal, the company has continued to tweak the Pulse, filtering its supply chain by specific localities, including new information on suppliers' financial health, and improving other features. The company is also continuing to move toward greater regionalization of production, especially in sensitive medical and technology sectors. Moreover, less reliance on China is likely to continue, reflecting customers' desire to have goods produced closer to their final destination.

Looking Forward: Increasing Digital Flow in a Post-COVID World

As more people transition to working from home, the need for effective information flows, improved data quality, and improved decision-making approaches will become more important than ever. Events such as the global pandemic will happen again, although perhaps not at the same scale. But in an increasingly volatile global ecosystem, they are inevitable. Creating a system of real-time visualized data requires a creative approach, or as Tom Linton calls it, "combining curious with crazy." Developing innovative data visualization approaches requires creative people who can express their vision to their leadership team and get buy-in. The changes required to move to a digital culture are discussed below.

Organizations will need to establish new ways of operating that focus on velocity of decision-making and free flow of information. This may cause much discomfort in some organizations where data is traditionally held very tightly. However, in the post-COVID world, organizations that do not shift to the new reality will suffer. In the new reality, measurements done once a quarter will not cut it. Cash is hiding in materials in all parts of the supply chain, and freeing up cash flow will be critical to ensure daily or even hourly responses, as the Flex case study shows.

Second, mapping one's supply chain using both automated and human intelligence will become critical to creating an immune response to future disruptions. In effect, layers of protection are being added to the supply chain by understanding where material is in motion and where it is being stopped in its tracks.

Third, supply chain visibility must extend down multiple tiers, and secure technologies will need to transmit information instantaneously up and down the tier. Blockchain is certainly a technology that can do this, but having reliable data transmitted in real time across an extended supply base will become more important than ever, as we have seen when a disruption in one part of the world ripples everywhere. This will happen even if corporations move suppliers to be more local to their customers. Future technologies will embrace predictive models, which can provide increased intelligence about the meandering flows of multi-tier supply chains. Early warning systems using artificial intelligence will be able to detect small discontinuities or events occurring multiple tiers away to enable early identification of issues.

Finally, our research shows that enabling smaller suppliers and tapping into the intelligence of individuals within smaller companies will allow companies to be more responsive and better able to withstand changes in the environment. This will require development of individuals to absorb data and make decisions using real-time information, including statistical literacy and sense-making. In the final chapter, these elements are extended into a view of what the supply chain will look like in the future.

CHAPTER SEVEN

Future Supply Chain Flows

We believe that the future lies in predictive analytics – to be able to see what is going on right now, and predict based on that data. Things are moving much faster than ever, are more real time, and the human reaction to something going wrong is too slow to stop the issue from turning into a major problem. Thus, we need to find a way to apply AI and science to a trend while it's occurring in the earliest stages – to be able to see that there is a path that is leading to something that will be terribly wrong, but to "see" it before it becomes impactful. Some of these things are glaringly obvious, but others are not. How do we use data to determine which events are on the path of going wrong?

Senior technology officer at a large technology company,
February 27, 2020

The Japanese have a famous proverb, *nana korobi, ya oki,* meaning, "Fall down seven times, get up eight." The proverb represents the idea of not giving up, but more than that, it doesn't start with falling down. It counts the first time you get up, reminding us that we have to show up first, in order to have the chance to fail, and then have the chance to get back up again.

Wabi Sabi, 2018[1]

The words of the senior technology executive, uttered just before the COVID crisis began its rampage, certainly ring true. The second quote, much more philosophical in nature, reflects the fact that we live in an imperfect world, but that our experience enables us to continue forward despite all odds. Sadly, we have not yet been able to master using artificial intelligence or digital analytics to predict the future, but we continue to learn from our experience.

In the early weeks of the COVID pandemic, the University of Washington began to make predictions about the epidemic and how it would affect people's lives across the country. Some of these predictions were accurate, others less so. In general, managers will not be able to predict how disruptive events all over the world will shape their company's environment, but by employing the concept of flow as a guidepost, they may be better able to manage them when they do. Just as the constructal law identifies how rivers will shape the landscape and how animals will have an impact on the ecosystem, the physics of flow can help us better predict how the global economy will look post-COVID. In this chapter we offer predictive insights from experts, along with some of our own, derived from many discussions.

Prediction 1: Global supply chains will converge locally in a post-COVID world.

As Dr. Bejan notes in his book *Freedom and Evolution*, understanding evolutionary design is central to understanding the current and future state of supply chains. Nothing moves unless it is driven. Once a natural system moves, its configuration continually flows toward the lowest point, pulled by gravity. As systems evolve, grow, and become more efficient, they also become more complex. Why? Because joining and moving (flowing) together requires less power than moving individually. This phenomenon is explained by economies of scale and social organization. Just as river systems evolve into small tributaries that flow into a major river, the economy, the life movement of a population, also flows in a hierarchical flow architecture.[2]

But how do we relegate ourselves to the idea of working and living normally after sheltering at home for two years (and counting)? How will global supply chains transform themselves as a function of the natural evolution of supply chains? And how can we operate in a world where there is so much uncertainty? Sudden and major disruptions are often the catalyst for change, as history has shown.

As an illustration, perhaps one reason many Western governments were so woefully unprepared for the COVID crisis is that we live in a period of peace, and global uncertainty was relegated as a thing of the past. The earliest supply chain systems were created as part of military forces assuring their preparedness for war; the science of logistics originated in the military, dating from the US Revolution and the Napoleonic Wars in Europe, and continued to evolve during the US Civil War, World War I, and World War II. When war was on the horizon, countries often began by creating stockpiles and grew the ranks of their armies through conscription. Even before the Pearl Harbor attack in 1941, the US military was marshalling resources. It seems as if preparedness for wars and pandemic events are cyclical, and every era revives the concerns and designs of past similarly horrible times. After an extensive period of peace, we neglected to prepare when the

COVID warning signs were on the horizon. We hopefully will re-emerge much more prepared for future health crises as a result of the difficult lessons learned during this pandemic.

Another example of the disruptive nature of change is the emergence of air freight to speed up supply chains in the last 40 years. This dates back to a sudden surge in air freight in 1978, when President Ronald Reagan deregulated the American air-line industry, removing entry and pricing restrictions. One ef-fect of this switch from a government-regulated to a free-market industry meant that air travel prices dropped significantly. This made air freight a feasible and rapid channel for shipping goods, which also led to the creation of next-day delivery services such as FedEx. America's new policy initially was seen as an unnat-ural shock to the system, but Europeans soon copied the idea, leading to the modern air freight industry. Freedom of flow is one of the essential elements associated with a free society, in which people are free to do as they choose.

The evolution of distribution channels in the United States is likewise changing. For example, Amazon's distribution centers have become condensed and closer to population centers to es-tablish last-mile delivery. Amazon was founded as an online bookseller. What rocketed the company to its current size was an online platform that evolved into a massive, far-reaching sup-ply chain. Its scale of design also shifted from national to global. Though there are many calls for localization of supply, the natu-ral pull of low costs, which we discussed in chapter 3, may once again begin to appeal to decision-makers in the world economy.

The world will always opt for cheaper, less expensive choices. There are still many regions with lower-cost labor, including Vietnam, Eastern Europe, Bangladesh, India, and Mexico. Of course, much of the world's commerce will eventually trickle and expand to a large river flowing into and out of Africa. Africa now has 1.3 billion people, and the long-term view would be mistaken not to include this continent as part of the evolution of the global economy.

In our opinion, the flow and spread of the coronavirus will have a massive impact on the design of our globalized supply chains in multiple industries. COVID originated in and spread through China, then to Europe and the United States via the ease of air travel. When Europeans traveled to the United States, the virus flew across with them. People who could afford to travel abroad were hosts that allowed the virus to travel. As China's business and operations infrastructure has expanded into every country, it is easy to see how COVID spread rapidly across the world. China's broad expansion is part of its Belt and Road Initiative to develop infrastructure and invest in Africa and elsewhere; the spread of the virus was a by-product, if you will, of the flow of global commerce. When the virus first appeared, people had no idea about what was happening or how the situation would escalate. The medical community was late in understanding the need for masks and social distancing. A human lack of awareness, translated on a global scale, became a global disaster: a six-foot spread radius, repeating itself over and over.

What will happen to the global supply chain over time? We are confident that we will soon see a reactionary movement to localized supply chains. In North America, the United States will remain focused on marketing and capital, Mexico on low-cost manufacturing, and Canada on natural resources. This evolution toward specialization has been a case of hits and misses. Specialization worked well in countries such as Ukraine, which capitalized on agricultural production and export. In the Warsaw Pact countries, the idea was to move manufacturing to Eastern Europe and Czechoslovakia, with the other countries producing food. However, every country in the Warsaw Pact wanted to produce the same products, especially cars and steel. This desire did not allow for specialization and comparative advantage, which we discussed in chapter 4, and ultimately led to failure and economic collapse.

A move toward localization and specialization – in North America, at least – seems likely to occur. From our position in 2021, it will occur gradually, as flows of commerce begin to move closer to customers. One can observe how flow systems will evolve, including patterns such as higher education becoming more online and businesses having managers work virtually. But such predictive flows are not obvious to everyone, often due to the common human trait of resisting change.

One reason that points to a localized supply flow is that the United States has not amassed land since 1959, when Alaska and Hawaii joined the Union. Our economic flow will likely consolidate into a pan-American supply chain, leveraging new trade agreements with Canada and Mexico that allow access to rare earths, metals, water, low-cost labor, and other resources. Currently, more than 30,000 people make automobiles and pharmaceuticals in Mexico, and the United States imports precious minerals, forest products, and agricultural products from Canada. There is a lot of room for a North American political structure to emerge, and the supply chain will flow that way from this development.

This will likely occur because the United States hit the pause button for physical growth in 1959, and as the concepts of hope and freedom move to China, it too will need to change. The labor arbitrage that the United States enabled in China 30 years ago directed all of our production to that country. But today we are in effect entering a post-global world of change. When everyone rushes onto a dry plain, and then they are caught unaware by a flash flood, their success is finite. We saw this in Europe after the Berlin Wall separated Germany in 1961, and Eastern Europe was pulled into a vacuum that it was unprepared for. Similarly, the United States rushed into Mao's People's Republic of China, attracted by its low-cost labor markets, and now the equilibrium of Chinese and American salaries signals that the flood has run its course.

New opportunities are emerging for supply chains to flow and flood a different plain, including places such as Romania, Armenia, and Eastern Europe. This will likely lead to increasing industrialization and will bring life to an area currently without a strong industrial base. Western Europe may disappear as a growth economy, and manufacturing will expand into Eastern Europe and increase wealth in that region. Then there will be opportunities for expansion into Siberia and other parts of Russia. This will likely occur due to a natural evolution of human society: movement of life and of wealth. If obstacles are put in front of this movement of wealth, the supply chain evolution will flow around them. Supply chains have been global in nature since the time of the Chinese Silk road. The destiny of North America having a north-south flow (from the United States and Canada to Mexico) and Europe having a west-east flow (to Eastern Europe and Africa) is likely to continue. The ongoing movement toward air freight and air cargo will make it relatively easy for companies to ship products from Asia and Europe and allow many industries to expand in those regions.

This economic evolution is also being driven by the shortages of healthcare PPE and medicines that arose during the COVID crisis. The United States was already acutely aware of the risks of single product sources located across the ocean. It was also aware of the healthcare risks of depending on China for critical materials. COVID very quickly jolted the entire system of private-sector supply chains in Western countries. To this end, the idea of localization appears more appealing than ever, particularly for strategically important materials such as nuclear warheads, food, medicine, active pharmaceutical ingredients, and hospital supplies. During Rob Handfield's testimony to the US Senate on May 19, 2021,[3] he noted how the US medical system has been increasingly reliant on low-cost manufacturing from overseas sources, a trend that has been occurring for the last 30 years. Much of this activity has been driven by the continued pressure of the healthcare system to buy pharmaceutical products and medical supplies at the lowest cost. Medical supplies that were in short supply during COVID included surgical and N95 masks, gowns, latex gloves, catheters, single use tubing, Propofol, IV fluids bioreactor bags, and many other items.

Beginning as early as the 1970s, many companies moved their manufacturing to low-cost regions because labor is often one of the highest contributors to the cost of goods sold. Offshoring was enabled by international trade agreements struck between nation states, reductions in duties and taxes, and other government incentives. The offshoring of production often meant that firms established large centralized production facilities to exploit volume advantages in locations such as China and India. Final products were manufactured in centralized facilities and then shipped around the globe to large distribution centers in the United States and Europe.

Many distributors of these products, including companies such as Cardinal, McKesson, Owens and Minor, Premier, MedAssets, and others bought them in large quantities at discounts. They then sold them in bulk to hospitals, based on contracts that promoted a "stack 'em higher, buy 'em cheaper" mentality. This practice was also encouraged by the Centers for Medicare & Medicaid Services and private insurance companies to reduce patient costs in hospitals. For products such as nitrile gloves, there emerged near monopolies, including Top Glove and Viet Glove in Vietnam. For N95 masks, more than half of the world's supply came from China, and in fact, much of that was produced in the Wuhan region where COVID originated. 3M secured all of its raw materials for masks from China, and its factory in that country was directed by the government to sell only within China through April 2020.

In pharmaceuticals, as more common products became generic, many of the inputs for drugs, known as *active pharmaceutical ingredients*, were sourced from India, which sources many of its materials from China. Manufacturing is outsourced to contract manufacturing organizations. These entities are often evaluated based on a per-unit-price basis and directed by brand pharmaceuticals to produce according to the "recipe" provided them using the suppliers they are directed to buy from. At the time of writing, bills are being introduced by Senator Gary Peters of Michigan and Senator Rob Portman of Ohio to reshore many of the critical hospital supplies the United States was short of during COVID.

COVID brought into focus American lives, not just American companies and their supply chains. Government agencies are suddenly discussing subjects such as stockpile inventory policies. They are also promoting investment for an industrial base that is capable of supporting localization and self-reliance. But there will be a balance, as localization cannot be made to occur even if a government wills it to happen. Natural forces will most certainly re-shape the flow of supply chains, but the economic decisions of managers and investors will be the greatest force in shaping how these supply chains evolve. Their responses will likely restrict the free distribution of technology and know-how, and intellectual property will be guarded much more closely. This will not signify the disappearance of global supply chains,

but rather a move to a more industrially segmented and thoughtful approach to supply chains than in the past.

This post-global world will result in a flattening of global commerce, and the calculus of lowest total cost flows will ultimately
determine how this flattening and leveling process will occur
over time. The movement and geography of people may shift
as a result of these flows. A de-globalization trajectory, based on
total cost increases in the East, will cause demographic change
across many regions. We may witness a pan-American highway
(PAH) – from Prudhoe Bay, Alaska, to Ushuaia, Argentina – begin to emerge as a challenge to China's Belt and Road Initiative.
This PAH will emerge as a novel strategy for the Americas: to
produce a North to South America economic power.

So-called belt and road initiatives may also emerge elsewhere –
a railway traversing Africa from Sudan to Dubai could one day
materialize. This railroad would circumvent the Suez Canal, sav-
ing several days of shipping time. This relatively small acceleration in the supply chain would have a huge impact on working
capital and generate millions of dollars. The project itself would
take a lot of time, of course, and would involve an expensive
infrastructure overhaul, as two gauges of railway currently link
northern and southern Africa. Also, Sudanese tribes would likely
oppose a railroad cutting across their land.

The constructal law is paralleled in the work of Richard
Dawkins in his 1976 book *The Selfish Gene*.[4] He argues that evolution is gene-centered – that a gene's purpose is to survive, at any
cost, regardless of the good of the group or the survival of the
species, as earlier scientists believed. Dawkins notes that genes
are in this sense "selfish," and the most aggressive will dominate. However, smaller or less aggressive genes do continue to
thrive as the larger genes with longer life spans exist. This phenomenon of the genetic realm is also true in the economic realm:

larger companies will likely "win" or remain dominant but will continue to support smaller firms. While at first glance dominant companies' support of weaker companies appears altruistic, it is in fact self-serving: each part of the ecosystem relies on the other to survive. Economic symbiosis is predictable and critical, so large corporate leaders should design their supply chains to ensure the survival of SMEs.

The Need for Digital Dexterity and Closer Supplier Relationships

We predict that future historians will view our era as pivotal in several arenas. First, the COVID pandemic has signaled the death knell for the analog world. With essentially everyone working from home, we are learning how much we can accomplish digitally. The push and pull between the analog and digital business worlds has been going on for 25 years: now, the internet is a critical public utility that serves as the foundation for commerce.

At the turn of the twentieth century, the horse and buggy and the automobile co-existed for at least two decades. This produced innumerable disasters until the slower, less efficient mode finally got left behind. Is this the horse-and-buggy moment for the supply chain? We think so, and that is a good thing. We can leave behind all the technologies, mindsets, and business structures that have persisted only through force of habit. A very basic example is how Excel spreadsheets are a relic of a time when we could not yet access and monitor supply chain information in real time. Tools such as the Flex Pulse – which integrates demand, inventory monitoring, manufacturing, quality, outbound transportation, and delivery – demonstrate that it is possible to aggregate and interpret live streaming data from multiple sources throughout the supply chain. Every supply chain should have a live ticker like this, and every company needs to prepare for these era-defining shifts.

The need for real-time information has never been more obvious than during the rapid succession of events caused by the COVID crisis. Indeed, some digital tools already have been adopted following this effort, such as the digital control towers monitoring COVID cases in many countries. It is time for everyone to get on board with real-time responses to issues. From here on in, digital dexterity will separate the winners from the losers.

As we anticipate the possibility of a new global recession, it will be useful to think about what we learned during this crisis and what it means for the future. First, COVID was unlike any other global recession or disaster, although our historical record of supply chain and global disasters confirms our hypotheses in *The LIVING Supply Chain* that real-time systems will become a ubiquitous requirement for success. The 1995 earthquake in Kobe, Japan, primarily had an impact on first-tier supply chains. This occurred during a pre-internet era, and it began to initiate greater work around supply market analysis and commodity strategies in a deeper way.

The 2000 dot-com bust, followed by the 9/11 terrorist strike, brought the term *resiliency* into our vocabulary as executives started to explore how to shockproof our supply chains. In 2008, an economic crisis demonstrated that events that were not in our direct line of sight could lead to severe consequences. This realization pushed procurement executives to take a macro view to help them understand these forces and how to plan for them. This typically meant conducting more category strategy reviews and increasing collaboration and communication with suppliers.

The next major event was the Thailand floods in 2011. The fact that 80 percent of hard disk drives were manufactured in

Bangkok resulted in a multi-quarter disk shortage for the computer industry. Then, later in 2011, the Fukushima earthquake created a tsunami, resulting in the disastrous flooding of a nuclear power plant that affected multiple tier-1, -2, and -3 electronics and semiconductor suppliers. The supply shutdown highlighted the industry's lack of deep supply chain mapping and extended visibility tools to drive multi-tier insights – most organizations had very little visibility beyond their tier-1 suppliers due to the limitations of these tools. These disasters led us to the shaping of where we are today.

The avalanche of economic stressors during COVID resulted in multiple bankruptcies across many sectors, particularly in SMEs. To survive, businesses needed six to 12 months of cash on hand; however, Bloomberg reported that 65 percent of Chinese SME companies had less than two months of cash.[5] The demand for these businesses is lost forever; since demand is perishable, these losses will never be recouped. If a long recession follows the COVID crisis, many of these smaller companies will run out of cash.

The takeaway here is that larger companies must rethink their position relative to smaller suppliers. To keep their supply chain intact, it is necessary to "pay it backwards." Larger companies need to take care of the suppliers that are the lifeblood of their supply chain. Managers should comprehend just how fragile a time we are living in and how dependent businesses are on upstream suppliers. Supply chain executives should pay careful attention to the limited ability of these small players to survive the current crisis. With little to no income for weeks or months, these businesses can go under quickly. After all, even well-capitalized global companies can be shut down when a tier-2 or tier-3 supplier goes under. For example, Aptiv, one of the world's largest automotive suppliers, announced in late March 2020 that it would draw down its entire $1.4 billion credit facility. Without your suppliers, where would your own company be?

As the COVID pandemic produces more variants and disruptions continue, more companies will likely experience financial distress. It might help to think of the supply chain ecosystem as a huge coral reef. Coral needs microscopic algae (zooxanthellae) to survive. But this algae cannot live above a certain temperature, so as the ocean warms, the algae dies. Without its food supply, the coral also dies. Large companies participate in a similarly symbiotic relationship with their suppliers. Without these smaller businesses to feed them, the whole supply chain ecosystem is dead in the water.

How, then, can an enterprise help keep its suppliers fiscally viable? Many strategies have already proven successful. For example, during the 2008 recession, Tom Linton, then with LG Electronics, became concerned about the small second- and third-tier suppliers. He persuaded his CFO to put together a pool of money to offer these suppliers as low- or no-interest loans. These are similar to the economic stimulus loans the US government gave to small businesses affected by COVID.

Linton was able to pull together $40 million in cash as a backstop for critical suppliers in the supply chain. The company accelerated payments to these suppliers and waived its original contractual payment terms in order to help these small suppliers survive.

Other companies took actions: Lockheed Martin advanced more than $50 million to SMEs in its supply chain,[6] and the telecom company Vodafone committed to paying its European suppliers within 15 days.[7]

Simply understanding what suppliers' capabilities are and what they need to keep afloat, through an open and honest dialogue, is important. Some suppliers may not want to disclose their financial difficulties for fear they will be cut off. The reality, however, is that everyone is facing financial difficulties, and the tipping point is often much closer than most leaders think. It is a mistake to rely entirely on a Dun & Bradstreet report or to assume that a company's direct, first-tier suppliers will take the initiative to monitor and manage critical lower-tier suppliers. We do not often think to bring CFOs into these conversations, but doing so is critical for the fiscal sustainability of supply chains.

Some first-tier suppliers may object to having their customers reach out and speak to second-tier suppliers (which first-tier companies think of as their own suppliers). However, power in supply chains flows toward the customer, and sharing the power may be necessary when suppliers create a barrier between your organization and what you need to know about your supply chain. After all, it is your financial flows that sustain the tier-1 and tier-2 suppliers. Keeping in mind that suppliers may be reluctant to reveal that they are about to fail, it is prudent to initiate honest dialogue from the top, to elicit feedback that can drive the chain-sustaining actions. In cash situations, large companies may need to request a supplier's financial records.

In the thick of a crisis, it is difficult for many executives to think about a recovery. However, we all need to think about preparedness for emergencies and ensuring a rapid recovery from whatever crisis comes into our path. Recoveries always come, and the slower they are in coming, the more damage is wreaked on the global economy. In 2008, worldwide government stimulus programs allowed stock markets to bounce back in six months, but the US and European economies did not recover for about 18 months. Now, in the dragging long-term pandemic recovery period, is the time to talk about what went wrong, what is still going wrong, and how to fix it. That may mean enhancing the power of sourcing or fixing upstream supplier problems, such as an inability to diversify a supply base.

We have in a sense become trapped into relying on current suppliers that are located in distant countries. When exports were restricted, many firms were powerless to recover because they had not established any other sources of supply. We were often forced into single sources in the first place due to choices we made in the design phase of product and service development, which restricted our options. Instead of using industry-standard components and statements of work, we allowed engineers to dictate components for which the specifications were too narrow, making it difficult to find alternative production sources. We specified building materials that forced us to buy from certain suppliers at certain times. Scopes of work were written in such a way that only a single company could produce a customized proposal.

The solution? Establish a means for dual sourcing. This will reduce procurement risks and costs. The pandemic has exposed the vulnerabilities inherent in global supply chains, and a new structure is likely to emerge. An implicit assumption in the press is that COVID caught everyone by surprise and that executives who foolishly ignored the risks of outsourcing to China are now paying the price. However, noted scholars and epidemiologists have been warning us of pandemics since the SARS virus. Pundits would further posit that in their pursuit of low-cost production, global corporations made naive assumptions that nothing could disrupt them. To this way of thinking, government-imposed tariffs were simply a passing political inconvenience, while Brexit restrictions would somehow be negotiated away by Brussels in subsequent years.

As we discussed earlier in this book, we have an alternative viewpoint: the major disruption of the global economy, including COVID and its effects, is a function of events that are part of the natural evolution of supply chains. Organizations that buy into this hypothesis need to design supply chains that are more agile to respond, design, and contract with multiple local sources of supply and that have a monitoring system that can provide early warning of disruptions on the horizon. These characteristics can lead to a new type of supply chain design, one that possesses the characteristic we call *supply chain immunity*.

In a recent conversation, economist Jason Schenker shared his insights on what lies ahead for the economy.[8] His outlook was that as more people work from home, organizations will realize their employees are just as productive working remotely. Adding to a firms' incentive to maintain remote work is that their ecological footprints also will be reduced, as fewer people will be driving to work, using space in a building, and consuming energy.

From a supply chain standpoint, Schenker predicts governments will take action. US congressional inquiries and government mandates in other countries will call for increased local production of medical devices and a clampdown on long supply chains in countries that are not close friends. This will be a national security issue, and may result in changes around local production in the United States and Western Europe for critical industries.

In an interview with *The Economist*,[9] Tom Linton hypothesized that we are entering a post-global world. Although this prediction implies a dark and menacing future, from a supply chain standpoint, it could be heralded as great news. One of the first laws of supply chain, as we discussed in chapter 2, is that proximity matters. The closer things are together, the faster and more efficient supply chains are, and the more cash flows through the supply chain. You might wonder why China became a critical supplier to the United States and Western Europe. Costs are like water: they naturally flow to the lowest point. So, as costs equalize around the world, it becomes more economically viable for companies to manage their supply chains regionally. "Post global" might have a negative connotation from a political perspective. But for the supply chain, it implies continued, growing demand for mass customization, which combines the flexibility and personalization of custom-made products with the low unit costs associated with mass production.

Prediction 2: Supply chains will reconfigure, but reshoring will not happen for all products and industries.

Will Western countries permanently move out of China in a post-COVID world? Well yes, somewhat … but it is complicated. The World Trade Organization published an interesting graphic that depicts a tremendous shift in the balance of trade between 2000 and 2017. Germany, Japan, and the United States were the epicenter of global trade, with Germany largely the industrial hub feeding Europe, Russia, Ireland, Turkey, and Eastern Europe. The United States exported primarily to Canada, Mexico, and Brazil. Japan was the industrialization center for Asia and Southeast Asia. China, just emerging as an industrialized country, had limited exports to Pakistan and Hong Kong.

In fall 1999, Rob Handfield traveled to Shanghai with a group of General Motors executives who were set on establishing production facilities in partnership with Shanghai Automotive to produce Lincoln Town Cars. During that visit, he observed the rudimentary condition of many factories but also the hunger to learn from large Western enterprises and to create a uniquely Chinese industrial base. On subsequent visits in 2004 and 2005, he noticed the rapidly increasing sophistication and change in the industrial base and the emergence of an upper-middle-class group of executives who sought to expand global trade. During this period, China rapidly became the center of the global economy. China is now the primary exporter to North America, Japan, Brazil, Russia, and most of Southeast Asia. Germany and China have a strong mutual trade balance, with Germany excelling in engineered products and biopharmaceutical manufacturing. Meanwhile, the United States has become a large importer of manufactured goods and has lost a good part of its industrial base.

In general, the world economy has risen because of globalization, so we cannot summarily dismiss the current model. Hundreds of millions of people have been lifted out of poverty – not just in China – and many lives have improved due to the fall of the Berlin Wall. As people rise up against globalization, the economies become more self-sustaining. For example, China is producing more products for China. That is good news for the economies of many countries, so post-globalization may not be such a bad idea.

In the past, the United States had to buy everything in China and import it because Chinese products were simply cheaper, and the flow of supply chains dictated that this was more efficient. In a post-COVID supply chain, however, Chinese exports have become much more expensive; transportation lead times have become longer, which drains cash. Companies will experience pain in the localization process, but it is good news for supply chain managers and for economies struggling to rebuild local businesses after COVID's path of destruction. Distance and proximity matter, and there is cost associated with change, but the result is a more economically efficient world.

In a post-COVID economy, we may witness multinationals shifting manufacturing out of China, but they will have a hard time accomplishing this on a wholesale basis. In recent years, we have already seen the move to produce goods closer to the point of consumption. Some companies that serve customers in North America, for example, will be more likely to transfer their production capabilities out of China than to ship products and materials back and forth.

But this does not mean that China will suddenly lose a large part of its industrial base. China will develop its own regional supply chains, which will benefit its companies, consumers, and economy. We believe more US companies will build factories in China to move closer to their Chinese customers, and more Chinese companies will move closer to their US customers. We predict increased regionalization of supply chains closer to their source by 2027. This may be expedited by regulatory shifts calling for localization of critical components for military support, hospital supplies, and medical devices as a result of the shortages seen during the last pandemic.

One of the positive outcomes of the COVID crisis is the increasing recognition of the importance of supply chain management in the national agendas of countries all over the world. The number of COVID deaths globally has engendered a serious "re-think" about how organizations and people do their work, and this obviously includes supply chains. For example, in April 2020, then Democratic presidential candidate Joe Biden said he felt that the United States needed a "coronavirus supply commander" to coordinate distribution of critical COVID treatment supplies across the 50 states.[10]

"This public health crisis is foremost a human crisis, but it is also a crisis of supply, logistics and distribution," Biden said. "States, hospitals, and health care providers should not have to bid against one another, or against the federal government, to get the supplies that they desperately need."[11]

Biden's comment suggests that this issue is rising to the top of national political mandates. However, a major shift in how procurement and supply chain professionals do their jobs and view their supply chain ecosystems will be needed. One of the first things we need to do is "blow up" our landed cost assumptions. Our 2019 views on total cost are not applicable in 2023; they need to change overnight.

In short, we are at a tipping point on Chinese trade. In this new reality, procurement executives will need to reexamine their assumptions on single and sole sources, and how many eggs they have in one basket. They also need to determine how many first-, second- and third-tier single sources they have. As we have seen, it only takes one bottleneck to shut down an entire supply chain, so diversity in supply will be paramount. We also have seen that in an economic crisis, all contracts are essentially obsolete. Old contracts should be terminated and rewritten. The healthcare and pharmaceuticals industries are making an entirely new set of assumptions about what is acceptable in terms of risk and what constitutes an immune supply chain. Everything we did last year, and will do next year, from a business and personal standpoint will need to change if we are to survive.

Prediction 3: Companies will not rely on force majeure but will increase agility to respond to supply chain disruptions.

Many legal experts expected to see an increase in the calling-out of force majeure in major contracts following COVID, but this has not materialized. It is unclear whether this crisis is truly an "act of God" that a force majeure stipulates. That said, a record number of force majeure certificates are being issued in China for companies caught not satisfying customer standards for healthcare supplies and other materials.

Chinese statutes define force majeure[12] as

> Any objective circumstances which are unavoidable, unforeseeable, or unsurmountable – article 180 of civil code. "Failure to perform the contract due to force majeure, or others, shall not bear any civil liability."

Companies have to be careful at how we look at force majeure. Every law is different in every country, and important to
understand.

> Alternate definition: Force majeure is a legal term under which a
> party may be relieved from liability for non-performance when
> "acts of God," such as floods, earthquakes, tsunamis, drought,
> government restrictions or other extraordinary circumstances
> beyond the party's control prevent fulfillment of contractual
> obligations.

How such terminology will be interpreted in the courts will
likely lead to many billable hours as lawyers argue over whether
COVID qualifies as a force majeure. Many states also have different definitions of force majeure, which may be the subject of legal
debate and argument.

A crisis is an opportunity for renewal. This is a great time for
procurement to expand its role in crisis management, to partake in
war room and pandemic response exercises, and to influence how
we operate in the new global economy. We have an opportunity
to rewrite the playbook, establish a new basis for sourcing products and services that support our economy, and develop a more
self-sufficient and resilient network in a post-global economy.

We are witnessing a disturbing trend: countries during COVID
reacted defensively, seeking to protect their own populations,
especially by hoarding respirators, masks, and other medical
supplies. When a foreign government steps in to shut down a
company's supply chain, it is time to rethink assumptions about
how supply chains are designed. Refusing to export medical
supplies commissioned by another country is a fear-based sup-
pression of market flows; some will exploit these dangerous conditions for their own profit and wealth.

Buyers will always be on the lookout for lower prices, and we are likely to see prices for many goods and commodities continue to remain volatile based on the ebb and flow of demand and availability. Locking in contracts for the next six months may be a typical strategy, but may also lock in suppliers to situations that are untenable. To be effective and agile in the face of uncertainty, multi-tier visibility tools are required to be competitive. If COOs or CEOs do not know what is going on in their supply base, now is the time to persuade them to invest in understanding potential risks and implementing processes to monitor, mitigate, and manage them.

It is also time to have more conversations about support for local suppliers and the communities proximate to our factories to mitigate risk and uphold company standards overseas. When demand drops, procurement is often pushed to make illogical choices. When CFOs want to delay payments to suppliers, supply chain leaders must insist that if we do not pay them now, they will not be there later.

Now is also the time to talk about how to manage the pull and push of on-hand inventory and price volatility. Shortages may recur when demand returns; get ahead of this, and discuss how to use cash for other purposes and to secure the future. If the company does not have a written statement about procurement controls sourcing, get that done now. It is also a good idea to establish a partnership with legal counsel and the CFO. Supply chain executives will need to establish policies and standards beyond force majeure, and they need to renegotiate bad contracts across the board. Commodities are sure to take some unanticipated hits. As the demand for oil trickled to nothing in spring 2020, prices dropped precipitously, which had a far-reaching impact on products and services including plastics, packaging, logistics, and energy. This drop in demand also provided an opportunity to look at how to lock in lower prices in anticipation of the future recovery. In light of commodity price volatility, it is time to establish contracts that can stabilize in the face of rapid shifts in markets.

Reassessing and strengthening relationships with people across the supply chain, from material suppliers to CEOs, is especially important now. One critical step is communication: reset supplier relationships, and have personal conversations with CEOs to align strategic plans with the current state of the supply base. Critical questions include: What are your needs? What are realistic expectations? How can we ensure job security for the key labor forces in our supply chain? Maintaining team relationships is also key: supply chain executives need to let people know that they are essential, and give them courage to deal with extreme uncertainty. When things change and people are not treated with respect and updated frequently, they will leave.

Another key step is to reassess the company's sourcing and engineering capabilities: Work with design and development right away to help populate materials. Now is the time to mitigate risk related to limited options in the supply base. Establishing a procurement engineering capability to mitigate single sourcing capabilities is essential.

Prediction 4: Successful companies will re-evaluate and rethink their relationships with critical suppliers.

Many executives we spent time with described how they were re-evaluating relationships with key blocs of low-cost countries that are suffering as a result of the pandemic. Consider the following situation: Recent reports and discussions with industry executives of factories producing the brands people wear every day reveal a dismaying state of affairs. In the middle of the

COVID pandemic effects in Europe and North America, many companies are cutting off the financial lifelines of their SME suppliers. For the last two or three decades, apparel manufacturers have outsourced all of their production to low-cost countries – first to China and later to Bangladesh, Vietnam, Sri Lanka, and India. In response to the coronavirus's huge impact on the global economy, apparel manufacturers (like many other sectors) are reeling and bleeding revenue and cash. In an attempt to stem the tide, many are cutting off payments to key suppliers in low-cost countries. In effect they are voiding contracts and employing force majeure clauses that in their minds relieve them of any responsibility, fiscal or otherwise, to key supply chain partners.

This is a dangerous game for all players. In a recent *Harvard Business Review* article,[13] Tom Linton and Bindiya Vakil emphasize that manufacturers should support the ecosystem of suppliers on whom they depend. Our research[14] shows that buyers who established regular risk-based performance reviews during the economic depression of 2008 were more likely to adjust payment terms and work with suppliers to improve cash flows of those facing financial strains. These actions had a profound effect by helping key suppliers stay afloat during the bad times and enabling them to surge when the economy bounced back. Even simple communications to check on the supplier's financial condition as well as instigating joint planning on business continuity measures can make a big difference.

For example, a survey shows that more than half of Bangladeshi suppliers had the bulk of their in-process or already completed production canceled after the beginning of the coronavirus epidemic.[15] When these orders were canceled, 72 percent of buyers refused to pay for raw materials already purchased by the supplier, and 91 percent of buyers refused to pay for the suppliers' production costs. As a result, 58 percent of factories surveyed were forced to shut down most or all of their operations. The result? More than 1 million garment workers in Bangladesh were fired or furloughed. Moreover, suppliers report that buyers are refusing to contribute to pay even partial wages for workers who are being sent home without being paid for work they have already completed. Disregarding contractual and purchase order terms, buyers were pushing out payments for orders they had already placed and were canceling orders that had been completed in Bangladeshi factories and were ready for shipment. They were canceling all orders that were already in the pipeline, many with commitments to raw material.

The results of such actions can create havoc for the apparel supply chain. Cancellations amounted to over $3 billion in business for Bangladesh, a country that relies on this industry to feed its population. Bangladesh produces almost $30 billion worth of apparel goods, about 10 percent of the garments sold to Western countries. One wonders: will there be an industry left to produce garments in a post-COVID world? Assuming the economy comes back, who will produce the millions of garments for the major brands producing low-cost apparel?

The International Monetary Fund (IMF) has begun to explore this issue, and many of the brands being investigated are making excuses and canceling orders with Bangladeshi suppliers. This includes brands such as Jones of New York, JCPenney, Kohls, American Eagle, and others. As a result, more than 2.7 million Bangladeshi workers became jobless overnight.

Incredibly, apparel makers have little legal recourse. Even though a purchase order is technically a legal contract, factory owners have been informed by their lawyers that they made a big mistake: those 200-page contracts contained small clauses that allowed buyers to cancel orders without notice. Factories do not have funds to pay legal teams to review these lengthy contracts and renegotiate them. It is not clear if these contractual terms violate the Uniform Commercial Code (UCC), nor are there funds to pay lawyers to examine them. The brands are powerful and have hired their own lawyers in Bangladesh to fight any claims. It is likely that the impact of these breaches of trust will last for years in the industry and may bankrupt large portions of the apparel supply chain.

At a minimum, brands should adopt fair and ethical contractual terms and use the following guidelines during a crisis such as COVID:

- Suppliers should receive payments for shipped orders. Buyers should ensure that payments go to suppliers to cover legally mandated wages and benefits incurred for orders already in production.
- Buyers who use clauses in their contracts to issue payment delays should help their apparel suppliers secure supply chain financing. Invoices can be factored through established fintech companies, allowing buyers to adhere to their purchasing contracts and pay suppliers for orders already in production or completed.
- Future procurement practices should focus on order stability for proper planning, timely payment of orders, and full respect for workers' rights.
- The IMF and other global agencies should mobilize international financial resources. Most garment workers and their families can be sustained for a few dollars a day. These workers depend on it.

We will likely see a very different apparel supply chain when business as usual begins. Suppliers will likely require a letter of credit from brands to ensure they are paid after delivery. This will pressure Western brands' cash flow and capital management, and will move the industry from a strategic partnership to a transactional model. This change may hamper or even set back the progress made by major global sustainability initiatives led by leading brands, such as the Sustainable Apparel Coalition. When brands do not take responsibility for their suppliers, suppliers will lose trust in brands' ability to ensure a living wage and workplace safety. Although survival of their brand is first and foremost in the minds of apparel executives, a more macro view of how to move past the COVID crisis should also be top of mind.

Guidelines for Accelerating Flow in Your Supply Chain

The primary responsibility of the supply chain remains, and will likely always be, managing cost. Executives still must decide when a primary focus on cost is appropriate and when other metrics such as cash flow and risk mitigation should be emphasized in decision-making. A supply chain manager's job is to find and collect intelligence on the market and evaluate this intelligence vis-à-vis the firm's objectives on cost, cash flow, and risk. The job is also to know where the market is now and where it will be in 90 days in order to move today at the market price or wait until later. The primary goal is to drive terms that will preserve the organization.

However, in today's "Hunger Games" environment, where every organization is looking out for itself and individuals are lining up for vaccine and tests, cost has become less important than simple survival. It is important to maintain a long-term view and understand that the changes we put in today, the infrastructure we invest in, and the organizational culture that we establish will have lasting effects on the ability to survive and compete on another day.

For this reason, establishing an enterprise that flows, evolves to changing conditions, and adapts accordingly is more important than ever. By putting in the right management systems today, we can establish a means for creating order from chaos. We can also establish governance mechanisms that create discipline and purpose in the decisions made by managers and workers in a company's ranks. This is a critical element for survival in the current environment. Supply chains left to react on their own will create greater chaos, and establishing principles for flow will enable supply chains to operate that much better in the face of chaos.

Only a handful of companies – including Apple, Google, Amazon, and Microsoft – have $100 billion or more in cash reserves, which they would need to survive an economy with no demand. Companies without these reserves need to rely increasingly on supply chain managers to create a more immune and agile supply chain, one that can flow and evolve with change. We hope that the guidelines and discussions contained in this book can provide a pathway for improved decision-making and the adoption of new technologies that can speed up decision-making and safeguard the lives of human beings worldwide.

These important guidelines for accelerating flow are shown in figure 7.1.

A set of policies establishes agreement on the general flow of how data is exchanged and made readily available to individuals across disciplines and operating units in the organization, and across key partner enterprises in the supply chain. As we have discussed, establishing a common set of standards for visualizing data is important, but even more critical is overcoming objections to sharing data. There is a perception, certainly within

FIGURE 7.1. *Guidelines for accelerating flow in your system*

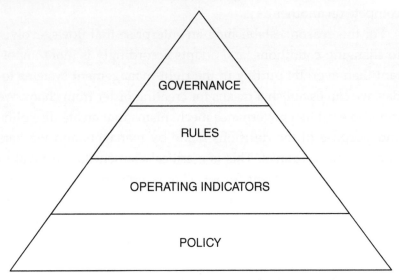

the legal community, that sharing information is risky and can expose the organization to litigation and liability. The consequences of not sharing data, compared to the risks, are much greater in our view. Companies that do not share information will not survive in today's cut-throat competitive environment and will not be around to fend off lawsuits.

Policy guidelines should focus on who is responsible for designing the system of data so it flows to the right people, and ultimately on who is approved to input data into the system. Policies should also hold people accountable for entering high-quality, accurate, reliable data. As we said earlier, shining a light on poor-quality data will resolve the problem quickly, as those held accountable will react to the attention. A central coordinator for enterprise data flows can ensure that information is getting to the people who need it in a timely manner and in a form that is actionable.

A second set of guidelines must be established around how operating indicators are represented, how they are calculated, and who is accountable for them. All parties must be aligned on how to measure flow and the visual indicators that represent whether inventory is moving through the system, processes are functioning efficiently, deliveries are occurring on time, and customers are getting their orders. It is a good idea to employ simple indicators, such as the ones that Flex employed in the Pulse, using red, yellow, and green colors to show the status of operating flows. For example, in the Pulse, red indicated that inventory for an item had been held more than 90 days (stuck in the system), yellow was 60 days of inventory (friction in the system), and green was 30 days or less (good flow). Similarly, indicators of process lead time showed whether problems were occurring. Red indicated more than 30 days to process an order, yellow was 20 days, and green was less than 10 days. Everyone should agree on these criteria so the indicators become universally employed and displayed on people's mobile phones, and everyone knows how material is flowing in the supply chain. Having the right user experience is key, so customer satisfaction measures can also be flowed back to ensure that everyone is aware of what customers are experiencing at the end of the flow.

The rules of flow provide insights as to how problems should be addressed, as well as the parties that need to be brought together to solve issues quickly. Friction in flow will inevitably occur, and the more quickly the members are brought together to solve the problem, the more likely it will be resolved. From the outset, the rules are not intended to assign blame but to gather the right decision-makers quickly to review the data, assess the situation, and agree on a course of action. The governance team needs to keep a committed focus on refining the rules and policies to address change, while building technical rules and components to continuously improve the application of these rules appropriately.

The governance of flow involves a high level, cross-functional council or management team. The team needs to meet periodically to review operating metrics and critical decisions that require a major shift in the design of flow systems and judge how well the application of the rules are working in the supply chain. The role of the governance council is to listen to the issues and provide a resolution that will ensure that that a decision is rendered to improve the problem at hand. The team must listen to different parties' perspectives, but ultimately it should be guided by the data flow indicators, which provide evidence of what happened. Then the team needs to assign accountability for any friction that exists and create a set of directives for resolving the issue.

A final set of guidelines for accelerating flow begins with a focused set of metrics; don't try to build indicators for the entire end-to-end supply chain. Begin with a limited set of processes, starting with the major flows in the system. For instance, do you want to improve your balance sheet or income statement, or do you want to focus on the overall customer satisfaction levels or customer experience? Let these objectives drive the problem, and start with those flows first, before you expand to others. You will learn as you move forward and discover the best route for improvement.

Be sure to invest the time upfront on proper training so the system is easy to use and people are encouraged to use the new flow indicator platform. Capture the user experience, and make it a pleasant and interesting one. Once people get used to using an app or reviewing performance indicators, their old habits and reliance on Excel spreadsheets will drop off.

Finally, minimize manual interventions in the system. Wherever possible, automate, integrate, and communicate the objectives. Manual overrides are the anti-thesis of flow, and are equivalent to putting more rocks in the middle of the stream, impeding flow. Do not be afraid to adopt new technology.

Moving forward to increase flow in the supply chain will take courage and vision, important elements of being a leader. We hope that you are successful in your journey to accelerating flow in your enterprise. If you focus on flow, the financial metrics will follow.

Notes

Preface

1 F. Greene, "Why Entrepreneurs Don't Learn from Their Mistakes," *The Wall Street Journal* (December 1, 2019), https://www.wsj.com/articles/why-entrepreneurs -dont-learn-from-their-mistakes-11575256081.

2 D. Finkenstadt, R. Handfield, and P. Guinto, "Why the U.S. Still Has a Severe Short-age of Medical Supplies," *Harvard Business Review* (September 17, 2020), https:// hbr.org/2020/09/why-the-u-s-still-has-a-severe-shortage-of-medical-supplies.

1. Supply Chain Flows and Immunity

1 "The Immune System," Johns Hopkins Medicine, accessed January 3, 2022, https://www.hopkinsmedicine.org/health/conditions-and-diseases/the -immune-system.

2 D. Finkenstadt, R. Handfield, and P. Guinto, "Why the U.S. Still Has a Severe Shortage of Medical Supplies," *Harvard Business Review* (September 17, 2020), accessed January 3, 2022, https://hbr.org/2020/09/why-the-u-s-still-has-a-severe -shortage-of-medical-supplies.

3 Y. Sheffi, *The Power of Resilience: How the Best Companies Manage the Unexpected* (Cambridge, MA: MIT Press, 2017).

4 Examples include *Big Data Driven Supply Chain Management* (Pearson Edu-cation, Inc., 2014) by Nada Sanders, which provides a five-step roadmap for leveraging big data and analytics to gain competitive advantage from your supply chain.

5 Yossi Sheffi books published by MIT Press include *Supply Chain Resiliency* and *Logistics Clusters* (2012). We have read both of these books, and agree that while supply chain resiliency is interesting, it sounds very expensive. This is because it

implies redundancy, extra inventory, and extra resources so that you can predict when and where risk is going to strike.

6 *Supply Chain Network Design* by Michael Sanders and Sara Lewis focuses on strategic supply chain network design and cites companies that have achieved cost savings from their supply chains.

7 W. Hopp, *Supply Chain Science* (Long Grove, Il: Waveland Press, 2011).

8 A. Bejan, *The Physics of Life* (New York: St. Martin's Press, 2016), 14.

9 E. Durschmied, *The Hinge Factor: How Change and Stupidity Have Changed History* (New York: Arcade Publishing, 2000).

2. Time, Velocity, and Immunity

1 Bejan, *The Physics of Life*, pp. 181–90. This quote has been modified from the original quote, "From science comes foresight, from foresight comes action," p. 190, Bejan.

2 "How We Make: Flex Pulse® Supply Chain Visualization," Flex, accessed January 3, 2022, https://flex.com/resources/how-we-make-flex-pulse-supply-chain-visualization.

3 Durschmied, *The Hinge Factor*.

4 Resilinc, accessed January 3, 2022, https://www.resilinc.com/.

5 R. Handfield, "Excess and Obsolete Inventory: You're All Responsible for It!" Supply Chain Resource Cooperative, NC State University (November 6, 2017), accessed January 3, 2022, https://scm.ncsu.edu/scm-articles/article/excess-and-obsolete-inventory-youre-all-responsible-for-it.

6 A. Bejan and J. Pedar Zane, *Design in Nature* (New York: Anchor Books, 2012).

7 S. Mazur, *The Origin of Life Circus: A How to Make Life Extravaganza* (New York: Caswell Books, 2014).

8 Bejan, *The Physics of Life*.

9 Tom Linton presented these ideas in December 2019 at the 40th Bi-Annual Supply Chain Resource Cooperative meeting at NC State University. These questions are predicated in large part on ideas introduced in *The LIVING Supply Chain*, which emphasizes the importance of keeping material in motion.

10 The ROIC is the operating profit divided by the invested capital. It tells us how much money the company can generate with new capital by investing in profitable projects. R. Delant, "ROIC: Why This Is the Best Ratio to Find Attractive Stocks to Invest in," Seeking Alpha (January 27, 2020), accessed January 3, 2022, https://seekingalpha.com/article/4355948-roic-why-this-is-best-ratio-to-find-attractive-stocks-to-invest-in.

11 The GMROII metric can be calculated for any period and equals revenue minus cost of goods sold (COGS) divided by inventory investment.

12 S. Davis, "U.S. Manufacturing: Why 2020 Was the Bottom of a Long Decline," *The Wall Street Journal* (December 15, 2020), accessed January 3, 2022, https://www.wsj.com/articles/u-s-manufacturing-why-2020-was-the-bottom-of-a-long-decline-11608037200.

13 "COVID-19 Part II: Evaluating the Medical Supply Chain and Pandemic Response Gaps," U.S. Senate Committee on Homeland Security and Governmental Affairs (May 19, 2021), accessed January 3, 2022, https://www.hsgac.senate.gov/hearings/covid-19-part-ii-evaluating-the-medical-supply-chain-and-pandemic-response-gaps.

14 K.F. Reding and C. Newman, "Improving Critical Thinking through Data Analysis," *Strategic Finance* (June 2, 2017), accessed January 3, 2022, https://sfmagazine

.com/post-entry/june-2017-improving-critical-thinking-through-data-analysis/. Also see comments by Joseph Yacura, "'Critical Thinking' vs 'Advance Critical Thinking,'" International Association of Data Quality, Governance, and Analytics, accessed January 3, 2022, https://www.iadqga.com/critical-thinking.

15 O. Bossert, A. Kretzberg, and J. Laartz, "Unleashing the Power of Small, Independent Teams," *McKinsey Quarterly* (July 12, 2018), accessed January 3, 2022, https://www.mckinsey.com/business-functions/organization/our-insights /unleashing-the-power-of-small-independent-teams.

16 O. Salo, "How to Create an Agile Organization," *McKinsey Quarterly* (October 2, 2017), accessed January 3, 2022, https://www.mckinsey.com/business-functions /organization/our-insights/how-to-create-an-agile-organization.

17 K. Sneader and S. Singhal, "From Thinking about the Next Normal to Making It Work," McKinsey & Company (May 15, 2020), accessed January 3, 2022, https:// www.mckinsey.com/featured-insights/leadership/from-thinking-about-the -next-normal-to-making-it-work-what-to-stop-start-and-accelerate.

18 We interviewed an executive in charge of supply chain risk management who worked at GM during the Japanese earthquake and tsunami in 2011.

19 B. Oskin, "Japan Earthquake & Tsunami of 2011: Facts and Information," Live-Science (September 13, 2017), accessed January 3, 2022, https://www.livescience .com/39110-japan-2011-earthquake-tsunami-facts.html.

20 "Earthquakes," LiveScience, accessed January 3, 2022, https://www.livescience .com/topics/earthquakes.

21 N. Wolchover, "Timeline of Events at Japan's Fukushima Nuclear Reactors," LiveScience (March 17, 2011), accessed January 3, 2022, https://www.livescience .com/13294-timeline-events-japan-fukushima-nuclear-reactors.html.

22 Sheffi, *The Power of Resilience*.

23 Interview conducted with Ryan Arens, June 25, 2020.

24 The VOCSN critical care ventilator provides invasive, noninvasive, and mouthpiece ventilation. Designed to work in hospital, institutional, transport, and home environments, VOCSN delivers a comprehensive set of ventilation modes and settings to meet patient needs. The advanced unified respiratory system combines responsive leak and circuit compensation as well as precision flow trigger controls to enable comfortable breathing and accurate therapy.

3. Thermodynamics and Evolutionary Flow

1 W. Shih, "Is It Time to Rethink Globalized Supply Chains?" *MIT Sloan Management Review* (March 19, 2020), accessed January 3, 2022, https://sloanreview .mit.edu/article/is-it-time-to-rethink-globalized-supply-chains/.

2 Bejan, *The Physics of Life*, p. 2.

3 Bejan, *The Physics of Life*, p. 230.

4 M. Craven, A. Sabow, L. Van der Veken, and M. Wilson, "Not the Last Pandemic: Investing Now to Reimagine Public-Health Systems," McKinsey & Company (May 21, 2021), accessed January 3, 2022, https://www.mckinsey .com/industries/public-and-social-sector/our-insights/not-the-last-pandemic -investing-now-to-reimagine-public-health-systems#.

5 Davis, "U.S. Manufacturing."

6 J. Emont and Chuin-Wei Yap, "Companies That Got Out of China before Coronavirus Are Still Tangled in Its Supply Chains," *The Wall Street Journal* (March

8, 2020), accessed January 3, 2022, https://www.wsj.com/articles/companies -that-got-out-of-china-before-coronavirus-are-still-tangled-in-its-supply-chains -11583686996.

7 "COVID-19 Part II," U.S. Senate Committee on Homeland Security and Govnermental Affairs.

8 A. Bejan, "How a Single Principle of Physics Governs Nature and Society," Tedx-Talks, YouTube (December 12, 2012), accessed January 3, 2022, https://www .youtube.com/watch?v=MHdfDzGypFM&feature=youtu.be.

9 A. Hussain, "How to Get between Terminals at Harsfield-Jackson Atlanta International Airport," Upgraded Points (updated April 26, 2021), accessed January 3, 2022, https://upgradedpoints.com/travel/airports/getting-between-terminals -at-hartsfield-jackson-atlanta-international-airport/.

10 A. Marshall, *Principles of Economics* (New York: MacMillian, 1920).

11 T. Boehme, J. Aitken, N. Turner, and R. Handfield, "Covid-19 Response of an Additive Manufacturing Cluster in Australia," *Supply Chain Management: An International Journal* 26, no. 6 (2021): pp. 767–84, https://www.ingentaconnect .com/content/mcb/177/2021/00000026/00000006/art00009.

12 M.E. Porter, *Competitive Advantage: Creating and Sustaining Superior Performance* (New York: The Free Press, 1985).

13 H. Sun, R. Handfield, and L. Rothenberg, "Assessing Supply Chain Risk for Apparel Production in Low Cost Countries Using Newsfeed Analysis," *Supply Chain Management: An International Journal* 25, no. 6 (2020): pp. 803–821, https:// doi.org/10.1108/SCM-11-2019-0423.

14 M. Szmigiera, "Manufacturing Labor Costs per Hour for China, Vietnam, Mexico from 2016 to 2020," Statista (March 30, 2021), accessed January 3, 2022, https://www.statista.com/statistics/744071/manufacturing-labor-costs -per-hour-china-vietnam-mexico/.

15 N. Mandhana and Myo Myo, "Pandemic Crushes Garmet Industry, the Developing World's Path Out of Poverty," *The Wall Street Journal* (July 11, 2020), accessed January 3, 2022, https://www.wsj.com/articles/pandemic-crushes-garment-industry -the-developing-worlds-path-out-of-poverty-11594472400?st=thhilpanzk5f7yf.

16 DXM, https://www.projectdxm.com/.

17 R. Handfield, "Five Myths about the Supply Chain," *The Washington Post* (November 24, 2021), https://www.washingtonpost.com/outlook/five-myths /supply-chain-myths/2021/11/24/f439dbec-4ca1-11ec-b0b0-766bbbe79347 _story.html

18 J. Bunge and J. Kanag, "Meat Was Once in Short Supply amid Pandemic. Now, It's on Sale." *The Wall Street Journal* (September 20, 2020), accessed January 3, 2022, https://www.wsj.com/articles/meat-was-once-in-short-supply-amid-pandemic -now-its-on-sale-11600614000.

19 M. Huber, "Smithfield Foods to Close Sioux Falls Plant Indefinitely amid COVID-19 Outbreak," ArgusLeader (April 12, 2020), accessed January 3, 2022, https://www.argusleader.com/story/news/2020/04/12/smithfield-foods -close-sioux-falls-plant-indefinetly-amid-covid-19-outbreak/2978385001/.

20 M. Corkery and D. Yaffe-Bellamy, "Meat Plant Closures Mean Pigs Are Shot or Gassed Instead," *The New York Times* (May 14, 2020), accessed January 3, 2022, https://www .nytimes.com/2020/05/14/business/coronavirus-farmers-killing-pigs.html.

21 J. Bunge and J. Newman, "Tyson Turns to Robot Butchers, Spurred by Coronavirus Outbreaks," *The Wall Street Journal* (July 9, 2020), accessed January 3, 2022, https://

www.wsj.com/articles/meatpackers-covid-safety-automation-robots-coronavirus
-11594303535?mod=hp_lead_pos5.

22 Reuters Staff, "Beyond Meat Results Beat, Suspends 2020 Forecast on COVID-19 Concerns," *Reuters* (May 5, 2020), accessed January 3, 2022, https://www.reuters.com/article/us-beyond-meat-results/beyond-meat-results-beat-suspends-2020-forecast-on-covid-19-concerns-idUSKBN22H2UW.

23 D. Adelman, "Thousands of Lives Could Be Saved in the US during the COVID-19 Pandemic," *Health Affairs* 39, no. 7 (2020), https://www.healthaffairs.org/doi/10.1377/hlthaff.2020.00505.

24 D. Levine, "No, Mr. President, Healthcare Workers Aren't Stealing Masks. You Failed Them," *The Wall Street Journal* (March 30, 2020), accessed January 3, 2022, https://www.washingtonpost.com/outlook/2020/03/30/low-tech-medical-equipment-saves-lives/.

25 R. Handfield, "Planning for the Inevitable: The Role of the Federal Supply Chain in Preparing for National Emergencies," Collaborating across Boundaries Series, IBM Center for the Business of Government (2010), accessed January 3, 2022, http://www.businessofgovernment.org/sites/default/files/The%20Role%20of%20the%20Federal%20Supply%20Chain%20in%20Preparing%20for%20National%20Emergencies.pdf.

26 R. Handfield, "We Need Supply Chain Immunity, Not Resiliency: A Position Paper," Supply Chain Resource Cooperative, NC State University (May 11, 2020), accessed January 3, 2022, https://scm.ncsu.edu/scm-articles/article/we-need-supply-chain-immunity-not-resiliency-a-position-paper.

27 "COVID-19 Part II," U.S. Senate Committee on Homeland Security and Govnermental Affairs.

28 "Blockchain Technology Is Set to Transform the Suppy Chain," Logistics Bureau (January 9, 2019), accessed January 3, 2022, https://www.logisticsbureau.com/how-blockchain-can-transform-the-supply-chain/.

4. Compression: The Localization of Supply Chains

1 S. Fox, J. Miller, and L. Meyers, "Seasonality in Risk of Pandemic Influenza Emergence," *PLoS Computation Biology* (October 18, 2017), https://doi.org/10.1371/journal.pcbi.1005749.

2 The UK Modern Slavery Act requires organizations to state the steps that they have taken during the financial year to ensure that slavery and human trafficking are not taking place in their supply chain or in their own business, or state that no steps have been taken. C. Camerlynck, "Are You Compliant with the UK Modern Slavery Act?" Tranparency-One (October 5, 2016), accessed January 3, 2022, https://www.transparency-one.com/compliant-uk-modern-slavery-act/.

3 The Australian Modern Slavery Act requires that organizations report annually on the risks of modern slavery in their operations and supply chains, as well as any actions taken to address those risks, such as due diligence and remediation processes. K. Tsai, "Australia Passes Modern Slavery Legislation," Transparency-One (January 8, 2019), accessed January 3, 2022, https://www.transparency-one.com/australia-passes-modern-slavery-legislation/.

4 The California law requires that covered businesses disclose on their websites their "efforts to eradicate slavery and human trafficking from [their] direct supply chain for tangible goods offered for sale – even if they do little or nothing at all to safeguard

their supply chains." K. Harris, "The California Transparency in Supply Chains Act: A Resource Guide," Office of the Attorney General (2015), accessed January 3, 2022, https://oag.ca.gov/sites/all/files/agweb/pdfs/sb657/resource-guide.pdf.

5 Source: Panjiva, part of S&P Global Market Intelligence. Data as at March 26, 2020. Provided to authors by S&P Market Intelligence.

6 J. Selin and R. Cowing, "Cargo Ships Are Emitting Boatloads of Carbon, and Nobody Wants to Take the Blame," Phys.org (December 18, 2018), accessed January 3, 2022, https://phys.org/news/2018-12-cargo-ships-emitting-boatloads -carbon.html.

7 G. Canon, "Ships Backed Up Outside US Ports Pumping Out Pollutants as They Idle," *The Guardian*, October 15, 2021, https://www.theguardian.com /business/2021/oct/15/us-california-ports-ships-supply-chain-pollution.

8 Emont and Yap, "Companies That Got Out of China before Coronavirus Are Still Tangled in Its Supply Chains."

9 A. Bejan, *Freedom and Evolution: Hierarchy in Nature, Society and Science* (Switzerland: Springer Nature, 2020).

10 J. Forrester, *Industrial Dynamics* (Waltham, MA: Pegasus Communications, 1961).

11 IHME COVID-19 health service utilization forecasting team, "Forecasting COVID-19 impact on hospital bed-days, ICU-days, ventilatordays and deaths by US state in the next 4 months," Preprint submitted to MedRxiv March 25, 2020, tracking ID MEDRXIV/2020/043752, accessed January 3, 2022, http:// www.healthdata.org/sites/default/files/files/research_articles/2020/covid _paper_MEDRXIV-2020-043752v1-Murray.pdf.

12 Source: Panjiva, part of S&P Global Market Intelligence. Data as at May 12, 2020. Provided to authors by S&P Market Intelligence.

13 Source: Panjiva, part of S&P Global Market Intelligence. Data as at May 12, 2020. Provided to authors by S&P Market Intelligence.

14 Interview, Fortune 500 manufacturer, SCRC Meeting, Raleigh, NC, December 2019.

15 Portions of this discussion are based on the following publication: R.B. Handfield, G. Graham, and L. Burns, "Corona Virus, Tariffs, Trade Wars and Supply Chain Evolutionary Design," *International Journal of Operations & Production Management* (2020), https://doi.org/10.1108/IJOPM-03 -2020-0171.

16 C. Roberson, "Comment: Coronavirus May Mean the End of Just-in-Time, as We Know It," TheLoadStar (March 23, 2020), accessed January 3, 2022, https://theloadstar.com/comment-coronavirus-may-mean-the-end-of-just-in -time-as-we-know-it/.

17 R. Handfield and T. Linton, *The LIVING Supply Chain: The Evolving Imperative of Operating in Real Time* (Hoboken, NJ: Wiley, 2017).

18 Handfield, Graham, and Burns, "Corona Virus, Tariffs, Trade Wars and Supply Chain Evolutionary Design."

19 Fox, Miller, and Meyers, "Seasonality in Risk of Pandemic Influenza Emergence."

20 H. Pearlberg, G. Tan, and P. Vercoe, "Blackstone Bets 18.7 Billion on Amazon Effect in Warehouse Deal," Bloomberg (June 2, 2019), accessed January 3, 2022, https:// www.bloomberg.com/news/articles/2019-06-03/blackstone-buys-18-7 -billion-u-s-property-assets-from-glp.

21 "BX:US," Bloomberg, accessed January 3, 2022, https://www.bloomberg.com/ quote/BX:US.

22 U.S. Department of Commerce, "Quarterly Retail E-Commerce Sales," U.S. Census Bureau News (November 18, 2021), accessed January 3, 2022, https://www.census.gov/retail/mrts/www/data/pdf/ec_current.pdf.

23 A. Berthene, "US Ecommerce Sales Rise 25% since Beginning of March," DigitalCommerce 360 (April 1, 2020), accessed January 3, 2022, https://www.digitalcommerce360.com/2020/04/01/us-ecommerce-sales-rise-25-since-beginning-of-march/.

24 https://www.bloomberg.com/news/terminal/PSI040MEWG77. Accessed January 11, 2022, by author.

25 https://www.bloomberg.com/quote/GLP:SP. Accessed January 11, 2022, by author.

26 R. Handfield, "SCRC Meeting Part 2: DH's Advanced Analytical Team Models Logistics Challenges," Supply Chain Resource Cooperative, NC State University (December 2, 2017), accessed January 3, 2022, https://scm.ncsu.edu/scm-articles/article/scrc-meeting-part-2-dhls-advanced-analytical-team-models-logistics-challenges.

27 D.K. Simonton, "An Interview with Dr. Simonton," in J. Plucker and A. Esping, *Human Intelligence: Historical Influences, Current Controversies, Teaching Resources* (2003), https://scholar.google.com/citations?view_op=view_citation&hl=en&user=gvsGBpoAAAAJ&alert_preview_top_rm=2&citation_for_view=gvsGBpoAAAAJ:hqOjcs7Dif8C.

28 Bejan, *Freedom and Evolution*, p. 17.

29 "Newton's Law of Gravity," Britannica, accessed January 3, 2022, https://www.britannica.com/science/gravity-physics/Newtons-law-of-gravity.

30 "Inside Huawei's Secret Plan to Beat American Trade War Sanctions," *The Economist* (September 11, 2019).

31 A. Fitch and D. Strumpf, "Huawei Manages to Make Smartphones without American Chips," *The Wall Street Journal* (December 1, 2019), accessed January 3, 2022, https://www.wsj.com/articles/huawei-manages-to-make-smartphones-without-american-chips-11575196201.

32 Fitch and Strumpf, "Huawei Manages to Make Smartphones without American Chips."

33 "Supply Chains for Different Industries Are Fragmenting in Different Ways," *The Economist* (July 11, 2019), accessed January 3, 2022, https://www.economist.com/special-report/2019/07/11/supply-chains-for-different-industries-are-fragmenting-in-different-ways.

34 "Supply Chains for Different Industries Are Fragmenting in Different Ways," *The Economist.*

35 R. Handfield, "Pharmaceutical Offshoring Makes Recalls More Costly with More Quality Headaches," Supply Chain Resource Cooperative, NC State University (July 16, 2018), accessed January 3, 2022, https://scm.ncsu.edu/scm-articles/article/pharmaceutical-offshoring-makes-recalls-more-costly-with-more-quality-headaches.

36 M. Smith, "Drug Recalls Put Spotlight on Drug Supply Chains," WebMD (November 19, 2018), accessed January 3, 2022, https://www.webmd.com/a-to-z-guides/news/20181119/drug-recalls-put-spotlight-on-drug-supply-chain.

37 Every particle attracts every other particle in the universe with a force that is directly proportional to the product of their masses and inversely proportional to the square of the distance between their centers.

38 Smith, "Drug Recalls Put Spotlight on Drug Supply Chains."
39 "Drug Shortages: Root Causes and Potential Solutions, 2019," U.S. Food and Drug Administration, updated February 21, 2020, accessed January 3, 2022, https://www.fda.gov/media/131130/download.

5. Freedom of Flow: The Adoption of Digital Dexterity

1   Bejan and Zane, *Design in Nature*, p. 83.
2   Bejan, *The Physics of Life*, p. 50.
3   F. von Hayek, *The Road to Serfdom* (Chicago: University of Chicago Press, 1944).
4   L. von Mises, *Socialism* (New Haven, CT: Yale University Press, 1951).
5   "Milton Friedman: In His Own Words" *The Wall Street Journal* (November 16, 2006), accessed January 3, 2022, https://www.wsj.com/articles /SB116369649781325207.
6   Bejan, "How a Single Principle of Physics Governs Nature and Society."
7   Bejan and Zane, *Design in Nature*, p. 87.
8   Bejan, *The Physics of Life*, p. 16.
9   "Gartner Says the CIO Is the Culture Change Agent to Augment Digital Dexterity in the Workplace," Gartner Press Releases (September 17, 2019), accessed January 3, 2022, https://www.gartner.com/en/newsroom/press-releases /2019-09-17-gartner-says-the-cio-is-the-culture-change-agent-to-augment -digital-dexterity-in-the-workplace.
10 L. Goasduff, "4 Ways CIOs Can Foster Digital Dexterity," Gartner (September 4, 2018), accessed January 3, 2022, https://www.gartner.com /smarterwithgartner/4-ways-cios-can-foster-digital-dexterity-infographic/.
11 R. Handfield, T. Choi, J. Venkatraman, and S. Murthy, *Emerging Procurement Technology: Data Analytics and Cognitive Analytics* (Tempe, AZ: Center for Advanced Purchasing Management, 2017).
12 S. Ransbotham, D. Kiron, and P. Prentice. "Beyond the Hype: The Hard Work Behind Analytics Success." *MIT Management Review* (March 8, 2016).
13 Deloitte Global CPS Survey. Accessed January 11, 2022, https://www2.deloitte .com/mm/en/pages/operations/articles/cpo-survey-.
14 Tejari.com, accessed January 11, 2022, https://www.jaggaer.com/tejari/.
15 Handfield, Choi, Venkatraman, and Murthy, *Emerging Procurement Technology*.
16 DAMA UK Working Group, "The Six Primary Dimensions for Data Quality Assessment" (October 2013), accessed September 3, 2020, https://silo.tips /download/the-six-primary-dimensions-for-data-quality-assessment.
17 G. Thomas, "How to Use the DGI Data Governance Framework to Configure Your Program." The Data Governance Institute (2014), accessed October 18, 2020, http://www.datagovernance.com/wp-content/uploads/2020/07/wp_how_to _use_the_dgi_data_governance_framework.pdf.
18 C. Stedman and E. Burns, "Business Intelligence," TechTarget, accessed January 3, 2022, https://searchbusinessanalytics.techtarget.com/definition/business -intelligence-BI.
19 "Magic Quadrant for Business Intelligence and Analytics Platforms," Gartner (February 23, 2015), ID:G00270380.
20 "Magic Quadrant for Business Intelligence and Analytics Platforms," Gartner.
21 International Institute for Analytics, "IIA Business Intelligence and Analytics Capability Report" (2016), accessed October, 2020, http://iianalytics.com

/analytics-resources/2016-business-intelligence-and-analytics-capabilities
-report.

22 International Institute for Analytics. IIA Business Intelligence and Analytics
Capability Report.

23 E. Durschmied, *How Chance and Stupidity Have Changed History: The Hinge Factor*
(Arcade, 2016)

24 Durschmied, *How Chance and Stupidity Have Changed History*.

25 R. Handfield, Siemens Building Technologies, Supply Chain Resource
Cooperative (December 30, 2018), https://scm.ncsu.edu/scm-articles/article
/siemens-bt-every-analytical-transformation-requires-a-jonah-hill.

6. Electrical Current

1 W. Manchester, *A World Lit Only by Fire: The Medieval Mind and the Renaissance:
Portrait of an Age* (New York: Little, Brown and Company, 1992).

2 J. Liker, *The Toyota Way* (McGraw-Hill Education, 2004).

3 See Chapter 2, "The Educaton of Michael Dell," in D. Salvatore, *Managerial Economics: Principles and Worldwide Applications*, 8th International Edition (Oxford
University Press, 2016), accessed January 3, 2022, https://global.oup.com/us
/companion.websites/fdscontent/uscompanion/us/static/companion.websites
/9780199397150/Additional_Case_Examples/Ch2.pdf.

4 Rossman, J., *The Amazon Way: 14 Leadership Principles behind the World's Most
Disruptive Company* (CreateSpace, 2014).

5 Durschmied, *The Hinge Factor*, p. 125.

6 "Decision Making in the Age of Urgency," McKinsey & Company (April
30, 2019), accessed January 3, 2022, https://www.mckinsey.com/business
-functions/organization/our-insights/decision-making-in-the-age-of-urgency
?cid=eml-app.

7 Return on investment.

8 Third Annual Data Governance and Quality Study, Supply Chain Resource
Cooperative, North Carolina State University, Raleigh, NC, December 2019,
https://scm.ncsu.edu/scm-articles/article/3rd-annual-state-of-supply
-chain-data-governance-report-released.

9 McKinsey & Company, "Perspectives on Transforming Cybersecurity,"
accessed January 11, 2022, https://www.mckinsey.com/~/media/McKinsey
/McKinsey%20Solutions/Cyber%20Solutions/Perspectives%20on%20
transforming%20cybersecurity/Transforming%20cybersecurity_March2019
.ashx.

10 CI, short for *continuous integration*, is a software development practice in
which all developers merge code changes in a central repository multiple
times a day. CD stands for *continuous delivery*, which on top of continuous
integration adds the practice of automating the entire software release process.
M. Anastasov, "CI/CD Pipeline: A Gentle Introduction," Semaphore (October 28, 2021), accessed January 3, 2022, https://semaphoreci.com/blog/cicd
-pipeline.

11 "2019 Supply Chain Data Quality and Governance Study," ivalua, accessed January 3, 2022, https://info.ivalua.com/hubfs/Ivalua_2019-Supply-Chain-Data
-Quality-and-Governance-Study.pdf?hsLang=en.

12 Elm Analytics, accessed January 3, 2022, https://www.elmanalytics.com/.

13 "Standard Definitions for Techniques of Supply Chain Finance" International Chamber of Commerce, accessed January 3, 2022, https://iccwbo.org /publication/standard-definitions-techniques-supply-chain-finance/.

14 A. Bloomenthal, "Basel III," Investopedia, accessed January 3, 2022, https:// www.investopedia.com/terms/b/basell-iii.asp.

15 Based on D. Lynch, "Business Unusual," *The Washington Post* (July 30, 2020), accessed January 3, 2022, https://www.washingtonpost.com/graphics/2020 /world/coronavirus-globalization-manufacturing/, and interview with Tom Linton.

16 At the time of writing, there are 21 factories in China.

7. Future Supply Chain Flows

1 B. Kempton, *Wabi Sabi: Japanese Wisdom for a Perfectly Imperfect Life* (UK: Piatkus, 2018).

2 Bejan, *Freedom and Evolution*.

3 "COVID-19 Part II," U.S. Senate Committee on Homeland Security and Govnermental Affairs.

4 R. Dawkins, *The Selfish Gene* (Oxford, England: Oxford University Press, 1976).

5 Bloomberg News, "Millions of Chinese Firms Face Collapse if Banks Don't Act Fast," Bloomberg.com (February 22, 2020), accessed January 3, 2022, https://www.bloomberg.com/news/articles/2020-02-23/millions-of -chinese-firms-face-collapse-if-banks-don-t-act-fast.

6 Lockheed Martin, "Statement from Lockheed Martin Chairman, President and CEO Marillyn Hewson on COVID-19 Reponse," March 27, 2020, https://www .lockheedmartin.com/en-us/news/statements-speeches/2020/statement-lockheed -martin-chairman-president-ceo-marillyn-hewson-covid-19-response.html

7 "Vodafone Launches Plan to Help Counter the Impacts of COVID-19," Vodafone, Press Release (March 18, 2020), accessed January 3, 2022, https://www.vodafone .com/news-and-media/vodafone-group-releases/news/vodafone-launches -five-point-plan-to-help-counter-the-impacts-of-the-covid-19-outbreak.

8 R. Handfield, "Outcomes from Our Post-Covid Seminar: Supply Chain Shifts, Leadership Communication, and a Rough Economic Forecast." NCSU Supply Chain Resource Cooperative, NC State University (April 16, 2020), accessed January 3, 2022, https://scm.ncsu.edu/scm-articles/article/outcomes-from-our -post-covid-seminar-supply-chains-shifts-leadership-communication -and-a-rough-economic-forecast.

9 "Supply Chains Are Undergoing a Dramatic Transformation," *The Economist* (July 11, 2019), accessed January 3, 2022, https://www.economist.com/special-report/2019/07/11/supply-chains-are-undergoing -a-dramatic-transformation.

10 Biden Harris Democrats, accessed January 11, 2022, https://joebiden.com /covid19/.

11 Biden Harris Democrats, accessed January 11, 2022, https://joebiden.com /covid19/.

12 Reuters Staff, "France: 'Force Majeure' Can Be Declared over Coronavirus in Contracts with Smaller Firms," *Reuters* (February 28, 2020), accessed January 3, 2022, https://www.reuters.com/article/us-china-health-france-economy/france -force-majeure-can-be-declared-over-coronavirus-in-contracts-with

-smaller-firms-idUSKCN20M1R8; Y. Yang, "Force Majeure in the Time of Coronavirus," ChiefExecutive (March 13, 2020), accessed January 3, 2022, https:// chiefexecutive.net/force-majeure-in-the-time-of-coronavirus/.

13 T. Linton and B. Vakil, "It's Up to Manufacturers to Keep Their Suppliers Afloat," *Harvard Business Review* (April 14, 2020), accessed January 3, 2022, https://hbr .org/2020/04/its-up-to-manufacturers-to-keep-their-suppliers-afloat.

14 M. Oliveira and R. Handfield, "An Enactment Theory Model of Supplier Financial Disruption Risk Mitigation," *Supply Chain Management: An International Journal* 22, no. 5 (2017): 442–57.

15 M. Anner, "Abandoned? The Impact of Covid-19 on Workers and Businesses at the Bottom of Global Garment Supply Chains," Penn State Center for Global Workers' Rights, Research Report (March 27, 2020), accessed January 3, 2022, https://www.workersrights.org/wp-content/uploads/2020/03/Abandoned -Penn-State-WRC-Report-March-27-2020.pdf.

Index

www.ingramcontent.com/pod-product-compliance
Ingram Content Group UK Ltd.
Pitfield, Milton Keynes, MK11 3LW, UK
UKHW040859140325
456137UK00013B/72/J